I've known Pastor Bob fo   t
began. His spirit of huml   :-
ing to say the least. I've continued to see the heart of a man who lives a life
exemplifying Christ. I'm proud to have been a small part of Pastor Bob's ministry knowing that it continues to touch lives worldwide. This book will live
on forever, and I trust that it will speak to anyone who reads it.

MICHAEL SWEET, STRYPER

Reading this, at the age of 36, made me realize that I, for the first time in
a long while, am onto something when I try to follow Christ. I'm not completely lost, like I thought I was—I just need to spend some more time with
Jesus! Bob has been a very important mentor to me, both in Extol and as a
leader in Sub Church here in Norway. The wisdom and teaching in this book
reflects a faithful servant's heart for God, and a man who stayed and continued when so many others left and disappeared.

DAVID HUSVIK, EXTOL

As I reflect back over twenty-six years of marriage, twenty-six years of walking
with JESUS and traveling to twenty-six countries I am full of gratitude for this
undeserved adventure. Although many have contributed there is one Pastor/
teacher that had the biggest impact on where I am today: Pastor Bob Beeman.

TRACY A. FERRIE, BOSTON

Pastor Bob has been a mentor and encouragement to me for many years. This
book is filled with valuable life lessons practically and spiritually. *Seriously?!*
is insightful, inspirational, and very real.

DUSTIN MARCELINO, DIRECTOR, "THE IDENTICAL"

Pastor Bob; a man who, through humility and transparency, has acquired a wisdom that he shares in love to bless, inspire and challenge everyone with a will to grow in their relationship with Christ and the freedom and joy it brings. *Seriously?!* is easy to read but takes a lifetime, in relationship with Christ, to comply.

ANDREAS LARSEN, SANCTUARY DENMARK

"Pops" has been a father figure, a doctor, a teacher, a mother-hen, a nutritionist, a friend and pastor to me for over 26 years. He's tempered my rough edges and taught me the important lessons of transferring The Word from my mind to my heart—and to just love. I wouldn't be here had God not brought him into my life, literally.

MATTHEW "MATCH" RAY, ACTOR

I have known Pastor Bob Beeman for over three decades. We met before Sanctuary was even formed and closely worked together once it did. Little did I know the impact this man would have on my life and ministry to this day. I love you, Bob…thank you for believing in me!

PASTOR NAR MARTINEZ

Pastor Bob has guided me from my band's first demo to the top of the Billboard charts. His wisdom has brought us through so many changes and challenges over the years and kept our eyes focused on Christ. We are now full time Musicianaries thanks to his godly counsel. Outside of family, no one has helped me more as a navigator through mountains high and valleys low in various chapters in my life than Pastor Bob. In fact, he's the reason I'm a pastor today—he ordained me! Regardless of your age, Bob's no nonsense nuggets of wisdom will make your road so much easier to traverse and help you avoid the pitfalls that ensnare so many of us.

MARK MOHR, CHRISTAFARI

I have had the privilege of working with Pastor Bob in ministry for over thirty years. He is a brilliant communicator and writer, and is very sensitive to the Lords leading. If I could describe Pastor Bob in a few words, it would be, "outside the box." This book is worth reading and I know you will find it fascinating.

JIM LAVERDE, BARREN CROSS

Pastor Bob has seen it all at this point—a lifetime of wisdom culled from decades of experience on the front lines is a priceless asset. He has spent his life helping others physically, emotionally and spiritually, so he has advice for almost every kind of situation. I'm thankful that he's sharing it with the rest of us!

MATT SMITH, THEOCRACY

For three decades, I have had the pleasure to call Pastor Bob my friend. He is the real deal: in his friendships, in his faith, in his knowledge, and talent for preaching, teaching, and writing - and in his heartfelt passion to help those who are going through a rough patch in life.

TED KIRKPATRICK, TOURNIQUET

Pastor Bob Beeman is much more than a pioneer of Christian rock music who helped blaze the trail for this generation. Pastor Bob is an exceptionally gifted communicator of the Gospel whose love for Christ and people is evident not only by what he says, but by how he lives his life. And he has the coolest voice I've ever heard. #MoveOverMorganFreeman

CHUCK TATE, PASTOR, ROCK CHURCH

SERIOUSLY?!

Letters to Myself at 21

PASTOR BOB BEEMAN

PUBLISHING

This book is dedicated to my parents
Marvin & Bonnie Beeman

Listen, my son, to your father's instruction
and do not forsake your mother's teaching.
They are a garland to grace your head
and a chain to adorn your neck.
PROVERBS 1:8-9

SPECIAL THANKS TO THESE VERY DEAR FRIENDS FOR THEIR CONTRIBUTION TO THIS BOOK:

Nannette Adair, proofreading and examination. "They say 'great minds think alike.' Thanks so much for your tireless efforts in helping me to think and rethink how I convey my thoughts. You always challenge me to communicate my heart more clearly!"

Eric Brown, cover photography. "You have an amazing talent for making your photographs come alive. Thanks for making me look good!" Check him out at ericbrownphoto.com.

Stephen Kuhn, layout and design. "Thanks for sharing my labor of love and making it look amazing!" Check out Stephens book, *10 Lies Men Believe about Porn* at www.beltoftruth.com

Starbucks in Hermitage Tennessee. "I appreciate you allowing me to set up my 'office' and write for a few months. Also thanks for making my 'Tall blond in a grande mug' before I even order it!"

To all my many friends internationally. You all know who you are and how much I love you!

CONTENTS

CAN I MAKE A FEW SUGGESTIONS?

have written this book in paragraph form, and I've placed each thought on it's own page. Besides simply reading the book all the way through, you can:

• Meditate on the truths of this book as a Daily Devotional.

• Use this book as a foundation for a study/discussion group.

• Adopt it as your personal journal, and express your thoughts in the blank space provided.

DEAR BOB AT 21...

t's been 41 years. 41 years since my 21st birthday. There are so many things I'd like you to know. So much that I've learned. So many mistakes that I wish you didn't have to make. And so much wisdom I wish you would've had at 21. I'm excited to write these letters to you. I've learned so much. I've come so far. And in many ways, I'm just beginning.

You think by the time you turn 62 you will be spiritually mature. You dream about being in the senior years of life and having so much wisdom. Now at 62, I've learned a lot about wisdom and I see how far I still have to go. I realize there's so much that I don't know. And I realize that the beginning of wisdom is the realization that I need Christ in my life and I need to let Him serve as my guide.

I remember being 21. You feel like you know everything. You don't think there is much anyone can teach you. You look at people with more age and maturity as being somewhat uninformed and unenlightened. You have the world by the tail, or so you think. At 62, I realize it wasn't true. I wasn't enlightened, I was ill-informed, and the world began to get very confusing. And that was the beginning of wisdom.

If I could summarize ministry at this point, I would simply tell you to live your life in front of people. Honesty. Integrity. Trust. Those are the keys. And that is where I will begin my series of letters to you. I want to encourage you in six different areas... Emotional, mental, spiritual, physical, sexual, and social. In my opinion, these areas define you. These areas work in harmony and impact each other.

I encourage you to stay humble, stay teachable, and dream big. Spend more time listening, especially to those who are older than you and have experienced more of life.

I'm looking forward to sharing these letters with you.

Pastor Bob

EMOTIONAL

"We accept the love we think we deserve."
STEPHEN CHBOSKY
The Perks of Being a Wallflower

What a great line from this book/movie. Not many statements about love are as true as this one. We grow up feeling that we don't deserve very much. We are taught that we have a "place" in society. We're told we are better than "those people," but not quite as good as "those others". Even though you were never told this while you were growing up, society has a way of putting you in your place. You have a big dream? There are those who feel it is their job to let you know you can never achieve it. You fall in love with a beautiful woman? Your friends are quick to remind you that she is "out of your league," and that you shouldn't even try to develop a relationship. There are those around you who have been abused and mistreated. As a result, they suffer from low self-esteem. They feel worthless. They settle for "love" in any way that they can get it. And their pain never goes away. In her book *"Men Who Hate Women and the Women Who Love Them,"* Susan Forward talks about men who abuse women. They are called "misogynists." Basically a man loves his wife, yet causes her tremendous pain because he acts as if he hates her. Confusing? Absolutely! And yet, the world is full of people like this. Their wives are convinced that this abusing husband loves her, and believes him every time he promises to change. All around us we see examples of limited love. But that is the great thing about being a Christian. It affords the opportunity to overcome 'limited love'. God demonstrates unlimited love. God is the instructor; He sets the bar, and shows you what love should be like. And as a result of your relationship with Him, you stop believing these self-destructive examples of love, and realize you deserve better. Your ideal for love is not set by the world around you, or by those who have demonstrated limited love. Your ideal is set by God's instruction. And His love should set the standard!

Don't be afraid of God's grace. Sadly, many churches these days are afraid of grace. They fear if they preach God's grace as the Bible describes it, that everyone will sin more and take advantage of the grace. So they continue to teach about sin and discipline, and warn people not to fall into these traps. They preach about God's unconditional love, yet avoid talking about His unconditional grace. Seriously?! I wonder where these guys are at in their personal relationship with God? Can grace be abused? From the world's and your point of view: Yes. From God's point of view, No. God's grace is unconditional. So what happens when you abuse grace and sin? God forgives you. And what if you repeat the same sin? God forgives you. You will learn this but I share now hoping the learning curve with shorten.

To live in grace is to enter into a partnership with God through his Holy Spirit. When you sin, the Holy Spirit instructs and teaches you, and points you back on track. If someone who calls themselves a Christian continues to sin without remorse or correction, he actually has a bigger problem than the sin itself. He has a problem with his personal connection with God. When Jesus spoke about the Holy Spirit, He said this: *"But when he, the Spirit of truth, comes, he will guide you into all the truth. He will not speak on his own; he will speak only what he hears, and he will tell you what is yet to come"* (John 16:13 NIV) He didn't leave this area of your life to your own abilities and strength. God knew we would fail if He did! His offer of unconditional grace in our lives is only possible because He also gives us His Holy Spirit to make it possible. Ephesians 4 tells us that our sin actually grieves the Holy Spirit. Let me summarize this thought once again. This is so important for you:

1. God gives us unconditional love and unconditional grace.

2. You cannot abuse grace by habitually sinning. Because the Holy Spirit lives inside of you, He will always make you aware of your sin and bring you to repentance.

3. If you have become insensitive to sin, you have a bigger problem than sin. You need to check your personal connection with Jesus.

Separate sin and guilt. From a very human point of view, we would like to see people do penance for their sins. We think they should have a "spiritual time out" and think about what they have done wrong and process it. While it is true that we need to learn from our mistakes, allowing ourselves to wallow in guilt is not the answer. Do you believe God needs to see your guilt, as if that justifies what you have done wrong? He doesn't. He already knows your heart. When you feel guilty, it keeps you from moving on in your spiritual life. It is difficult to feel God's love and forgiveness if you are beating yourself up in the meantime. Jesus died for your sins. That includes the guilt from your sins. His desire is to bury them "as far as the east is from the west." (Psalm 103:12 NIV) It is difficult to bury it if you are still focused on it! And what about others? Why is it that you want them to feel guilty for their sins? Why do you want them to suffer? Honestly, one of the biggest reasons is jealousy. That's right! Why should they be able to sin and get away with it, if you can't? The Bible outlines many things that will cause you to stumble and cool your affection for God. You know the list. You rehearse the list. And you try to live according to the list. And that is exactly what God asks you to do. He wants you to be an imitator of Jesus Christ. But… that doesn't mean that your desire for those things has gone away. Your flesh still wants to get involved in almost everything on that list! And when someone else commits those sins—and gets away with it—and is forgiven, you feel like you are being slighted. It isn't fair. Why should he get away with it and you can't? You think, "I would have enjoyed that sin too!" You forget the difficult part. Now he has to deal with his actions. The Bible says, "Sin pays its servants. The wages are death." (Romans 6:23 PHILLIPS) Don't forget about the aftermath. There is a deeper reward for following God and His principles. Sin only lasts for a moment, but the ramifications of the sin can go on for a lifetime.

Are you motivated by guilt or by freedom? At this point in your life, you are motivated by guilt. You feel guilty about your sin. You feel guilty about the course you are on. You feel guilty about your relationships. You feel guilty about your past. You feel guilty that you can't be perfect. You feel guilty about feeling guilty. Again, Christ came to give you freedom, freedom from guilt. He gave you His grace. And when you're truly living in His grace, you realize that His power and His authority in your life removes your guilt and shame. You're free because Christ set you free. It isn't something that you earned. It isn't something that you're good at. It's not even something that you're capable of doing. Being free is the position that He gave you. And He told you to celebrate it. So, choose freedom instead of guilt. Allow God to do everything in your life that He's promised to do. Only He can truly set you free. Guilt will take you on the road of mourning your past. But freedom will set you on the path to celebrate today and tomorrow.

God is not mad at you. It is easy to feel that way. It's especially easy when you make big mistakes that you have a difficult time finding forgiveness for yourself. Because you are disappointed in yourself, you incorrectly assume that God feels the same way. He doesn't. Your expectations involve perfection. You incorrectly assume that you are always going to get everything right and there shouldn't be any mess-ups. But God knows so much better. He expects the mistakes. He knows you are not always going to get things right. He's already planned for it through His death on the cross. That is what His death was all about, remember!? His death isn't a license to choose poorly. God expects you to do the best that you can. It simply means that He is there to help pick up the pieces when you do make mistakes.

Grace versus condemnation. When you really understand what grace is all about, condemnation has no place in our lives. And yet, condemning others is what many Christians around you choose. Seriously?! You know the ones I'm talking about. The "bullies" of the faith. They throw their legalism around like a knife, cutting and chopping up everyone who doesn't agree with them. They are self-appointed gate keepers—reminding you of your sins, and defining "the right path" from their limited perspective through the filter of condemnation and judgment. So the question becomes this: Is it possible to actually be a Christian and walk in the flesh? Yes. "Do not quench the Spirit." (1 Thessalonians 5:19 NIV) It is a difficult way to live, but some have hardened their hearts to the point where their focus is on their belief system and not on their personal relationship with Jesus. When that happens, they filter everything through their own emotions and understanding. They ignore the Holy Spirit inside, and have chosen to be dogmatic and unbending. Instead of allowing the Spirit to work in grace, they force their position through a legalistic mindset.

If you keep sinning, won't you eventually "fall from grace?" I think this is an interesting thought, since it presupposes two things:

1. You are in control of grace;

2. And because you are in control, you can fail—and fall.

Of course, these two statements are NOT true. Grace is a gift from God. It doesn't now, nor has it ever, been dependent on your ability to somehow keep it going. It is God's undeserved kindness to you!

Grace in your face! God's grace in your life depends on your response to Him. The extent that you show His grace to others will be in direct proportion to the amount of grace you have personally allowed God to show you. If you haven't received God's grace and allowed it to change you personally, you cannot give it away. That is why there will always be so many angry Christians around you. They are miserable. They are trying to live in a religion they cannot master, and they refuse to allow God's grace through His Spirit to affect and assure them. The only way they can survive and still feel good about themselves, as Christians, is to be dogmatic; they think that discipline is the way to God. They protest everything. Their list of "Christian offenses" grows every day. They become self-appointed guardians on the internet as they correct everyone's doctrine, and blast those with whom they don't agree. They are trolls. They are bullies. They are angry. Seriously?! Jesus says, *"I came that they may have and enjoy life, and have it in abundance (to the full, till it overflows)"* (John 10:10 AMP). What an exciting promise. Those whose lives are legalistic and condemning are to be pitied, not feared. They are actually missing the point: "For all have sinned and fall short of the glory of God" (Romans 3:23 NIV). "All" includes them!

Don't get so upset when people sin differently than you do! Have you noticed? We all sin differently. Most of the time, we are more aware of how others sin than we are of our own sins. Today's church has no difficulty condemning the gay movement or, well, fill in the _____. It's hard to keep up with the "sin-of-the-month" club. But then, they don't see the gossip and hypocrisy that goes on in their churches as a real problem. Seriously?! It is a real problem. Sin is sin. Until you understand that your sin is the same in God's eyes—and just as potentially destructive as anyone else's sin, you will continue to view it as "us" verses "them"—the sinners and the rest of us (the ones who sin differently.) We tend to measure sin by what is visual and can be seen. But what about the sins you practice in private? Sin is not just sin because others can see it. It is still sin when you are alone and no one is looking. And, conveniently, those are usually the sins the Christian community "forgets" to discuss. Their focus is only on the sins they can see. But why are we still talking about sin? We need to look past the whole issue of sin. Jesus paid the ultimate price on the cross so that we could look past sin and find unconditional love. Reminder: "It was while we were yet sinners that Christ died for us!" (Romans 5:8 NIV) If each of us were to pick up stones and throw them at sinners, you would get knocked down from the force of those stones thrown at you just like everyone else!

You are no longer a sinner! God has a new name for you: SAINT! In essence, you are no longer a sinner saved by grace, but now you are a saint… who occasionally sins. Why is that important to know? Names and labels are important. Imagine a child growing up with parents continually telling him that he is stupid. It actually happens too many times. That child usually grows up with major self-esteem problems. Being called a 'sinner' is horrible. Since Christ's death on the cross, you have a new identity and a new name. He doesn't want you to be identified by the "sinner" mentality any longer. He wants you to know that all things are possible for those who are in Christ Jesus. (Matthew 19:26) Take your position in Christ—the one that He gave you. And know that it is His gift to you, and his gift makes so many things possible!

Forgiveness is not a light switch. The pivotal point of the whole Bible is forgiveness. God asks you to forgive generously, just as he has forgiven you. But that is where it becomes difficult. There are people you dearly love. When they mess up, you have no problem forgiving them. You know deep down in their hearts that they didn't mean anything malicious. But what about those people who actually do? What about those whose only plan is to ruin you, to speak badly of you, and to even make up stories about you that aren't true? You will have a few of those people in your future. And when they attempt to harm you, you will find yourself harboring unforgiveness. Surely God doesn't expect you to actually forgive them, does He? Well… yes! But it may take you some time. Forgiveness isn't a light switch. You can't simply turn it on and off. At the end of the day, you can't flip the switches and say, "You're forgiven. You're forgiven. You're forgiven. You're forgiven." You will need to work through the forgiveness process first. You will have to figure out what to do with the feelings of betrayal and unfairness. It's okay to take the time you need to honestly be able to forgive. In my experience, sometimes it takes years. It doesn't mean that you are not spiritual enough and not trying hard enough. Some hurt just runs a lot more deeply than other hurt. But it is important that you begin the process of forgiveness as soon as you can.

Forgive and forget? Seriously?! That really isn't possible. And yet, you feel guilty when you are not simply able to wipe those offenses out of your mind. You brain doesn't work like that. You can't pretend the offense never happened. But honestly, you wouldn't want to. The very thing that keeps us from repeating our mistakes and from getting involved in the same unhealthy relationships is the memory of them. If we didn't remember our past difficulties and hurts, we would be vulnerable to repeat them over and over again. It would be a continuing cycle. You don't need the memories to disappear. You just need to replace them with the feelings that accompany forgiveness and move ahead.

Forgiveness and trust are not the same thing. God asks us to unconditionally forgive each other. But trust is a different issue. In fact, the
Bible warns us against blindly trusting people. A quick trip through
Proverbs will show you that trust is earned. It takes time to build, especially when the trust in your relationship has been hindered. Anyone in
a longstanding relationship, friendship or marriage, will tell you that
expectations are easily confused. Along with the confusion comes a
lack of trust. It seems that a lot of relationships are constantly in the
process of repairing trust. And so it should be. It is sometimes too easy
to dismiss an offense, and in doing so, never learning from it. Building trust in a relationship helps to understand each other even more
deeply, and to realize how all individuals in the relationship are in the
process of completing each other.

You want to save the whole world. That's great, but… It is a noble thing to desire salvation for all of those around you. But it is a very large task and one that you will not accomplish. Rather than praying, "Lord, show me how to single-handedly save the whole world with the amazing talents and wisdom that I possess," pray instead, "Lord, show me MY people. The ones you want me to love and commit to. The ones who will allow me to speak into their lives and the ones for whom I can make a difference." That won't be everyone. But it can be many. At 21, you have a burden for the rock and roll crowd. By the way, that is not going to change. But it is a very real burden for a very specific group of people. It doesn't mean that God won't give you a burden for others along the way who are not part of that particular crowd, but you can be sure they will continue to make up most of your ministry. For instance, when you are stopped at a traffic light and people are crossing the street, you will always notice the rockers more than anyone else. They automatically have your heart. While it is true that you need to be a light to the world, you will most likely have a special place in your heart for some very specific people.

Planning to preach to 1,000 people and only 10 shows up? It will be these times that really test your motives and your heart for people. You should have the same intensity for 10 as for the thousands. If your love for people and your burden for their spiritual lives is really from God's heart, then the numbers won't matter. You should honestly feel the same after a great meeting with 10 people as you would with 1,000 people. Some of it has to do with faithfulness. The Bible tells us that if we are faithful with the small things, He will be faithful to give us even more to care for. It is really up to you. Make sure your heart is pure and driven by his unconditional love for others.

There is a difference between building an empire and building the kingdom. God wants us to contribute to His kingdom. He wants us to follow the heart He's given us and the motivation He's provided within us. Personal agenda has no place in increasing God's kingdom. At 21, you don't understand the difference. You are still building an empire. You say you're doing it for God, and mostly that's true, but you have yet to grasp what building the kingdom is all about. It isn't about promoting a particular ministry. It isn't about defending a particular lifestyle. It's about inviting people to be part of the kingdom of God, no matter what they look like and what kind of music they listen to. It isn't sufficient to say that you're accepting of all people. You must act on it. Building an empire is exhausting. There's so much involved. And it is so easily toppled. But, building the kingdom of God is part of the collective. You're part of an international society of Christians. We all have the same task. There are enough pastors around building their little empires in their churches. Please don't be one of them. Always see the bigger picture. Always realize that it isn't about you. It's about Him.

Discover your passions! There are significant desires within you that motivate you. Music. Ministry. People. There are so many things for which you feel passion. Realize that those are God-given and for a purpose in your life! You will find there are two ways to tackle life. First, you can try to do it with discipline, forcing yourself to do what you feel needs to be done. So many spend their entire lives doing this. But it is a miserable existence, without a lot of reward and driven by obligation. If you are only motivated because you have this deeper sense that you "should" be, then you are operating by obligation rather than motivation and you will burn out before achieving success. But if you are motivated by your passions, you will not need to force yourself to be involved, and you will find a supernatural energy that remains consistent. At the end of the day, to be motivated by discipline will leave you tired and unfulfilled. But if you were motivated by your passions during that same day, you will find yourself with energy to spare and a deeper feeling of fulfillment and purpose.

Passion is God's gift to keep you motivated. It keeps you from burning out quickly. You struggle with this. You need to have new challenges and new passions all the time. You find it difficult to move ahead with anything if you lack the passion to do it. Many see lack of motivation as laziness. But I believe for most people, laziness is only a failure to discover the God-given passions inside of you. Once you find them, you will not lack in motivation. But be careful that you don't overlook them, or "spiritualize" them away. When God gives you a purpose, a specific area of ministry or people to involve yourself with, you will always feel a passion for it. This does not mean you are in the mood to work on that particular thing all the time. But passion for it will still be there.

You are currently involved in helping to pioneer Christian rock music. You feel the depth and force of that calling every day. It's your passion. Even though there are many people inside of the church who don't understand what you are doing and feel the need to condemn you for it. You have your eyes firmly on the vision for the future. You feel the passion for it more deeply than you feel the opposition. And at the end of the day, you are very excited for the ministry that is beginning through Christian rock music. Keep your eyes on your calling, and continue to allow your God-given passion to inspire and motivate you. Keep the vision for the future of what the ministry of Christian rock can become.

Stay dedicated to music "on the edge" no matter where the "edge" may take you. Music is a language for feelings. It's also a vehicle for the message. Continue to be excited that the message of the Gospel is being presented to a whole new generation in ways that they can understand. One of the dangers as you get older will be the tendency to judge music according to your own musical tastes. Some of the music in the future will be difficult for you, simply because it is very bold and unusual. After all, you grew up with Elvis Presley. Music in the future will be a giant leap forward from his mellow crooning. Remember, you don't always have to personally like a musical style for God to use it. And, you will find, when you keep an open mind, you will begin to enjoy a lot of music you never thought you would enjoy!

Stay true to yourself. Don't conform. Your confidence at 21 is huge, and God gave you that confidence to go with your vision. But the confidence is supernatural, NOT earned. That is actually a positive thing. You haven't yet been exposed to too many people who tell you how many things you cannot do. Therefore, it doesn't occur to you that you can't accomplish big things. My strongest advice to you at 21 is to keep your innocence in this area. Believe that big things can happen. Trust God for the impossible. Allow Him to increase your passions and motivations daily. Don't listen to those who try to tell you that your dreams cannot be accomplished, or that God is unhappy with your pursuits. Your confidence, which is grounded and motivated by the Holy Spirit, is healthy.

Remember to always dream big! Many of the goals and dreams you find in your heart will seem too extreme and practically impossible to do something about. The fear of getting started might seem paralyzing. In that case you will have to figure out what in the past has made you afraid of taking a leap toward something bigger. God is a God of possibilities. He will always put creativity and big ideas in your heart. Never fear them. Embrace them. Again, nothing is too big for God to handle. You may feel small and incapable, but in the hands of God, anything is possible. Don't limit yourself, and don't limit God. God is always dreaming bigger than you!

Don't be afraid of your emotions. Many spend their lives trying to avoid difficulties. But in the end, difficult times are inevitable. They are a part of life. When you encounter them, don't bury or stuff your emotions. As you process through your difficulties, you may find yourself more inclined to flee from them. But, if you do, you will discover later that the emotional problems you thought were behind you will come back and hit you even harder. Actually, many of your most important moments in life will be difficult. So when crisis hits, and it will from time to time, learn from it. It's healthy to continually be aware of the things that affect you and begin to bother you. Some emotions may even lead to depression. But what you learn from difficult times will have a profound influence on what happens to you in the future. Don't avoid those lessons.

Sometimes, something needs to die. We all react differently to certain feelings. Some people become suicidal while others simply become depressed. But for all of us, it's important that we figure out what's wrong. If you feel like something needs to die inside of you, let it! It will probably take some effort and maybe even some counseling before you detect the problem. But don't simply pretend that nothing is wrong. Again, these are the periods of your life that are of major importance. When you discover what's wrong, you can take the next step to freedom. But never kill yourself—simply kill whatever needs to die!

Sometimes life sucks. Sometimes your circumstances are unfair. Sometimes you will feel defeated and misunderstood. There will be times when you simply want to quit. Hang in there! Life is still worth living. Always get back up, and always keep trying. Success doesn't always happen the first time and not even the second time. It may take a few times before things actually fall in line. Sometimes we feel like the Christian life should go smoothly. In fact this concept is perpetuated in the modern church. We are taught that the Christian life is easy. It seems that most church leaders always look and act as if all is right and normal. Seriously?! This simply isn't the case. The breath of life is a blessing, but there are those days that just suck!

You will have bad days. Recognize them when they happen, and do whatever it takes to move past them. But, be careful that you don't make important decisions during a bad day. Everything will look different to you. Your counseling to others will not be pure and unbiased and even small decisions that you have to make will be clouded. When you have a difficult day, don't push it aside. Deal with it. Take some time to regroup. Breathe. Relax. Get back on track. Take a personal inventory and figure out what needs to be corrected.

Make sure your issues don't have issues. Because you are emotionally driven, it is so easy for you to take simple difficulties and blow them out of proportion. Small difficulties become larger when they remind you of other past hurts and disappointments. For example, when a friend shows up late for an appointment, or acts in a certain way that seems extremely disrespectful, this reminds you of all the other times he has been late, or acts in that same manner. You say to yourself, "If he were truly my friend, he would care more about our relationship and would show it by being on time." Then, at that point, his tardiness and actions remind you of other friends who have proven not to be very good friends. You begin to feel the emotional sting from those past failures. This pain attacks your very being. And then, since your friend is late or acts in a way that seems disrespectful, you have ended up feeling the weight of all of your past failed relationships. And now, you have just put your friend into a box, a box of failed expectations. When your friend shows up late, you are already upset with him. And he wonders why simply being late dictates such a massive negative reaction from you. "After all," he says, "I thought since we are such good friends that you of all people would understand the last minute demands we sometimes have." And he is correct. Be aware of those times when a simple issue is ready to explode and become something out of proportion. Separate your emotions and make sure to work through them one at a time and not in groups. The resolve for one small issue may not look anything like the resolve for another. And when you are emotionally charged and put them all in a group, you end up making the wrong decision.

God desires an honest emotional relationship with you. Voices throughout the westernized Christian community both warn about using emotions for your encounters with God AND encourage experiential emotional encounters. Both are very wrong to do! Who created your emotions? When Jesus described the greatest commandments as "love" based, He opened up a whole new dimension for our faith. No longer are we limited to outward encounters with God. His Holy Spirit inside of you now offers you "love based" fruit. You cannot really use them, unless you feel them. In fact, our honest encounters with God will increase our emotions. An emotionless encounter with God would quite honestly be a drag. God's desire is an intimate relationship with you. "

> And my language and my message were not set forth
> in persuasive (enticing and plausible) words of wisdom,
> but they were in demonstration of the [Holy] Spirit and
> power [a proof by the Spirit and power of God, operating
> on me and stirring in the minds of my hearers the
> most holy emotions and thus persuading them]."

1 CORINTHIANS 2:4 AMP

What defines a "real" man? The media paints a certain picture of what this man looks like. Ask anyone. "Who comes to your mind when you think of a "real" man?" Their answers would most likely include: John Wayne. Clint Eastwood. Chuck Norris. Bruce Lee. Brad Pitt. Denzel Washington. Pastor Bob. Well, maybe not that last one. But if we were to ask what defines a "spiritual" man, our answers would be quite different. And yet, the true measure of a man is not his physical appearance or his "sex appeal." The true measure of a man is in his devotion to God and his ability to transform that relationship into a lifestyle.

Once you have failed, get back up. You are not defeated. It is so easy to stay down when you get knocked down. That feeling of defeat plagues us all. The author of Hebrews says, "Therefore, since we are surrounded by such a huge crowd of witnesses to the life of faith, let us strip off every weight that slows us down, especially the sin that so easily trips us up. And let us run with endurance the race God has set before us. We do this by keeping our eyes on Jesus, the champion who initiates and perfects our faith." (Hebrews 12:1-2 NLT) They say that most millionaires have declared bankruptcy several times before they have their final success. You see it isn't how many times you get knocked down; it's about getting back up. Success is simply getting back up the final time. If you stay down, you will stay defeated. If you keep getting up, you will succeed at some point. We all make mistakes. You have plenty of them ahead of you. If you continue to learn from them, and use them as wisdom for the next time, you will find yourself successful.

Beware of those who tell you what to believe. They usually have an agenda. Rather, embrace those who share *how* to believe. These people will help you open the door for discovery. But it needs to be *your* discovery. No one can live your faith for you. Your faith is yours. Everyone's faith is different. We are all distinct members of the body of Christ. You will learn to really love the diversity that Christians have. Because we were all created in His image, we all reflect who God is in different ways. Therefore, you will learn so much about God through other people, and other people will get to know certain aspects of God through you.

You need to feel. You need to see. You need to experience. That is the whole reason Jesus came to earth in the flesh. He knew we needed to experience him and observe him. His desire was to be personal with us. Simple theology doesn't give us the room to experience God as we need to because "simple" isn't deep enough. God desires to go even deeper with us on a personal level. He doesn't just want us to know "stuff" about Him – He wants us to know *Him*. This is a major difference.

Don't be afraid to question your traditions. They are, after all, simply traditions. To compare the modern church to the first century church would be a huge contrast. And yet, we hold many of our modern traditions as holy and pleasing to God. You would be surprised to find the origin of many of our modern traditions. So many of them were born in paganism; they were simply borrowed by earlier followers of Christ, who had difficulty leaving their pagan symbols behind. The church building, the pastor's chair, stained-glass windows, the church steeple, the pulpit, even the Sunday morning order of worship had their origin in other belief systems. Your relationship is with Jesus, not with church traditions. Make sure that your communication with God and your representation of Him to the outside world is not built on tradition. Don't be opposed to tradition. But understand its place in your celebration of the faith. Also understand that to question your traditions is not the same as questioning your faith. Don't let it throw you into crisis. Tradition is tradition. Your personal faith should remain untouched by your conflict with traditional Christianity. There are many times where Jesus questioned the religious traditions of the organized church of His time, and corrected them.

Make sure you relate to God according to who he really is. So many people have decided to have God their way. They begin sentences with, "I believe in the kind of God that…" They decide what is best for themselves, and they play "build-a-God" with their theology. Seriously?! That's a little silly, isn't it? It's extremely unrealistic. But we do the same thing in our churches and in our theology. If we could possibly take our agendas out of our concepts of God, I am sure each of our beliefs would change drastically. But that doesn't happen. It is impossible to truly read the Bible without your own agenda. Just look around at how many churches and denominations there are around us. Each denomination, including non-denominational, has a little different belief system and all of them call themselves Christians. You need to do whatever you can to relate to and experience God according to what He says about Himself. That is where the absolute truth rests. So, do what you can to discover who God is and allow God to continue to show you the truth about Himself.

You often lose yourself in your pursuits. You imitate other people. You try to be someone that you are not. And in essence, you don't fully understand yourself and probably never will. This is why it's important for you to have intimate friends and mentors. You need people who can help you look inward. People who can help to identify who you truly are, the true you, people who see you through Gods eyes and help you. Allow friends and mentors access to keep you from getting lost or remaining lost. The body of Christ can help balance you as you pursue your passions and truth. When you feel you know all the "right" answers and yet not know how to live out those answers, you will need intimate friends. Without their influence, you'll find yourself just going through the motions, and never truly connecting with the one who made you.

You've been taught that you should study and stay on course. You've been taught that if it feels good it must be wrong. Seriously?! So, you run from emotions and feelings. You stuff them while you pursue honesty and truth. This is a big mistake and creates a huge gap between theory and practice. Allow God to encourage you through your intimate friends and mentors. Allow God to keep you on track in your pursuits.

e **afraid of depth.** Dare to go deep. Long to go even deeper. nd time reflecting. Contemplating. Sorting. Be quiet. Remember to have "sanctuary." Find a quiet place, your sanctuary, and make it a priority.

Make sure that those around you don't simply have an encounter with the church, but that they have an encounter with Jesus Christ. Jesus didn't come to simply replace a "System" with another "System". Jesus wanted to change our hearts. Jesus isn't creating an army, but He desires for us to love unconditionally. You need to practice feeling with your own heart, and seeing with your own eyes. Train yourself to listen to the Holy Spirit. He is the one that will guide you and help you blossom in these areas.

As you begin your journey as a pastor, don't take others problems too lightly. Allow God to give you passion and love for people. Don't look at individuals as projects with an easy fix, but remember that people are listening to your advice. If you simply give them instruction without helping them to find their heart for God, they will never be able to stand on their own. Their emotions will continue to betray them; therefore, guiding people is a tremendous responsibility requiring a deeper look into their situation before telling them what to do. There is never a quick answer. It is more about encouragement and giving them a direction. You will often find that something completely different and unexpected can generate the questions people are asking you.

Do you believe God can make a difference in your everyday life?
Does that sound like a redundant statement? It is one thing to believe
in God, but another thing to believe God. It is much easier to preach
Christian ideals than it is to actually live them. Anyone can preach
them. It just involves a little study and a lot of imitation. But to actually follow your sermons yourself, well, that is another matter. At 21,
I don't think you have yet found the connection between your ability
to live what you are teaching, and the teaching itself. It isn't your job,
as a Christian, to simply tell people what the faith is all about. That is
why the Bible tells us to be "doers of the Word, and not hearers only."
(James 1:22) There are so many around you whom you assume are
spiritual giants. They have lofty sermons. They appear super-spiritual.
You will see many of them fall in the next few years. Many fall from
moral failure. Some fall from a crisis of faith and others from exhaus-
tion. Why didn't they practice what they preached? Good question.
And why don't you? Your Christian life isn't about lofty thoughts and
ideals. Rather, it is about a concrete relationship with Jesus that continues to change your life. The way you live your life in front of people
will always speak more loudly than any sermon you can ever preach.
Remember: Your life IS your most important sermon!

God told you? Seriously?! Here is a phrase you use way too much. You describe how God is working in your life and the dreams He is giving you. "God told me to build this." "God told me to end that relationship." Really? You cannot assume that everything you feel, or think you feel, is from God. Every time you say, "God told me…" you enter sacred ground. People put stock in those words. They count on them as being from God. And if your "God told me" plans don't succeed, it not only causes you confusion it throws others personal relationship with God into confusion. There are many who claim God's stamp of approval on their projects and their direction. And when they don't succeed, they never correct it. They never say, "I must have heard the Lord incorrectly." They are usually on to the next "God told me." Be careful how you use that phrase. In fact, find other ways to say things. "I believe God is putting ___ on my heart" is a whole lot more truthful. And it allows for your imperfection in listening, instead of hinting that God is somehow changing His mind.

Allow others to express their faith differently than you do. For some, it is the traditions they grew up with that create the environment needed for them to find their intimacy with God. Just because some of those traditions were not born in the same revival and re-thinking that you are going through doesn't make them any less valid. That little grandmother who enjoys singing the same hymns that she has sung in church since she was a little girl should be allowed to continue doing so. When the young people come into the church and demand that they do away with the hymns in favor of more contemporary songs that they "enjoy," they do a disservice to the little grandmothers of the world who find their connection with God in another way. Your connection is not the only connection. Again, diversity is so healthy. There are so many things you have yet to learn from the little grandmothers of the world! When you see the effect of God's Spirit and grace in the lives of the older or more traditional church generation, you will find you still have much to learn!

The battle between wisdom and knowledge is never-ending. In many cases, they feel a lot alike. But their conclusions are worlds apart. The Bible tells us that, "… knowledge makes us proud of ourselves, while love makes us helpful to others." (1 Corinthians 8:1 CEV) Wait. Shouldn't the biblical comparison be knowledge versus wisdom? Actually, wisdom has very little to do with knowledge. Wisdom is an expression of a deep understanding of God's unconditional (Agapé) love for Him, others, and us. Wisdom sees the world through God's eyes. It listens to the world through His ears. And it feels the world through His senses. That's why wisdom will always seem elusive. Many study to find it. Others try to copy it. Still others feel that it is already a part of who they are naturally. But all of these miss the mark. Wisdom increases as your spiritual life matures. That is why, many times, you will find yourself understanding more about God's love from a crisis situation than you will from going through easier times. You will grow the most during those times when you are forced to rely on God rather than your own abilities. Wisdom is always born in love. Knowledge finds its foundation in your own experiences and your limited ability to process those experiences. Wisdom happens when you allow the Holy Spirit to filter through those experiences and teach you deeper meanings and applications.

MENTAL

Of all the things I've lost, I miss my mind the most.
OZZY OSBORN

You can allow your "tastes" to define you, but don't allow them to separate you. You are a "metal head." You are on the edge. Your taste in music pretty much defines your taste in clothing, art, and even friendships. Music will always be a driving and defining force in your life. That isn't going to change. You, at 21, have made a commitment to stay "on the edge wherever the edge takes you." That decision will take you to a lot of places you have not even dreamt about yet, and put you in situations you cannot even imagine at this point of your life. It is all very exciting! It's an adventure! You will connect with many people in the coming years who have the same heart and tastes that you have. You will find success as you continue to pioneer in the realm of Christian Rock/Metal music, even though, at times, it will cost you dearly. And your distress will come mostly from well-meaning Christians who truly believe you are "of the devil." They will tell you "the beat of the music is the same that is used to conjure up demons" or "you can't understand the lyrics" or "God's music doesn't sound like that, it is more mellow and utilizes church organs." Seriously?! There will be times when the "opposition" becomes so strong, that you will most easily find your sanctuary with those who believe and experience things the same way that you do. It's nice to feel that level of support and safety. But you need to connect with other kinds of Christians as well. Those outside of your comfort zone have a lot to teach you. Their life experiences may parallel yours in ways you don't yet understand. You will find that those who will mentor you the most will be outside of your normal comfort zone. Keep an open mind and an open heart to those God sends your way. Many will be cleverly disguised as opposers when, in truth, they are guardian angels! You will eventually learn a huge lesson: You don't have to agree with someone or like them for God to use them. You don't have to love their musical style for them to be close friends. That will even include Country Western music. But I am sure you have a difficult time believing that now!

You are in charge of your own moral condition. At 21, you have this feeling that you can still get away with a few things secretly. You push a few limits. You experiment in private. You have this sense that what you do in private will have no effect on your ministry or your friendships. You feel in control of your thoughts and emotions, and you believe you can change course or correct these issues anytime. You split your life into two categories: Those things that are "You" and those things that are "Not really you." You convince yourself that the "You" part will always win over and will be the part of you that people see. And the "not really you" is actually not part of you, and remains hidden from others. As you grow older, you will learn that BOTH of these define you. And those things that are "not really you" have defined you just as much as the 'you' parts. You have some difficult discoveries to make. And with these discoveries, you have to decide who you want to be and what you will do with those things that define you. There is no splitting. The concept that you can separate is mental gymnastics. In reality, it has always been completely "you" all along. The strength of your relationship with Jesus, the honesty with which you live your life, and the integrity of your moral condition will be significantly impacted by the decisions you make now.

The key to fighting addiction? Don't get started! So many of your friends are addicted to porn, cigarettes, and alcohol. Every one of them started with simple exposure, which became an addiction. My greatest advice to you at 21 about fighting addiction is very simple: "don't get started!" Stay a virgin. That will keep you from being tempted to sleep with as many girls as possible. Don't start smoking cigarettes. It's easy to stop smoking if you never get started! Set a limit to alcohol consumption. If you must drink, drink one beer and walk away afterwards. Don't watch porn. If it pops up on the computer without you doing anything, have the strength and the clarity of mind to close the page. That's a whole lot easier than fighting the addiction later on!

Fight the battle before the battle. Realize that you aren't as strong as you think you are. Even Billy Graham would struggle when put in the right circumstances. You are human. You don't have superhuman strength. You will find yourself tempted more than you thought you could be. And you may find yourself failing, when you thought you would succeed. Fight the battle before you even get there. Rehearse what you would do in these situations and let your reaction be automatic. For instance, if you've already decided what you're going to do when porn pops up on your computer, then you have no decisions to make. You've already decided to close the page. And if that's too difficult, you automatically turn the computer off and walk away. You must realize that you have limitations. Therefore, it's very important that you fight the battle before the battle even begins.

Many times we're tempted simply because "everyone else is doing it!" We feel like the odd duck in the room. And it's difficult to be the only person there who is not smoking, drinking, doing drugs, or hitting on women. We've seen the research, and we know that excess leads to addiction. We know that smoking cigarettes can cause lung cancer, and we realize the implications. But, in a social setting where everyone appears fine, all the research goes out the window. We join the ranks where "everyone else is doing it" and justify ourselves accordingly. God has a bigger plan for you! These temptations are the very things that will keep you from becoming all that you can be. Realize that acting on temptations creates barricades. "…but each person is tempted when they are dragged away by their own evil desire and enticed. Then, after desire has conceived, it gives birth to sin; and sin, when it is full-grown, gives birth to death." (James 14-15 NIV) Acting on temptations does not put you on the road to success. They will only harm, not help you.

You need to realize that you're an addict at heart. You're an over-achiever. You get hooked on things really easily. You made a decision to never touch alcohol. Stay with that decision. You made a decision not to smoke cigarettes and to stay a virgin. Likewise, you made a decision not to get started with porn. Hold to your resolve very strongly. Don't give in. Remember that these are the very things that you could struggle with in the future. You have all of the emotional and physical characteristics that could easily cause you to become an addict. Always remember that. And always allow God to steer you in another direction.

Legalistic accountability doesn't work. I see so many accountability groups for all kinds of things: porn, excessive drinking, drugs, anger management, etc. In my experience, very few people actually work through their problems in accountability groups. And if they managed to stay away from their problems, they seem to become addicted to the group itself. Even though support from other people does help, I believe God wants to set us free so that we don't continue to need support in the same area(s) over and over again. Religion uses legalistic accountability—based on performance. The focus is the undesired behavior and the performance necessary to change the behavior. I call it the pink elephant syndrome. We all still see the pink elephant (the behavior) in the room. We point to it. We talk about it. We pray against it. But it's still there. God's desire is to remove the elephant altogether. It's like telling everyone "don't think about the pink elephant." Seriously?! Of course, that's the very thing that causes people to think about it. We continue to struggle. Instead, we need to encourage each other. That is true biblical accountability; honest encouragement focusing on what God wants for each of us. It is then that we have an opportunity to model ourselves after Jesus and behave accordingly.

Jesus wants to set you free. The Scripture says, "it's for freedom that Christ set us free." (Galatians 5:1 NIV) It may be too difficult for you to get through your problems and addictions. But it's not too difficult for Him—it's His power that we need to rely on. When you encounter these things that are too large for you, it isn't a matter of you becoming stronger. It's a matter of letting Him become stronger within you. Once again, it's not about discipline. It's not about trading one addiction for another one. It's about surrender. It's about His strength within you. It's about His healing. With simple accountability, the root problems never really go away.

Repent! This is a misunderstood word that is thrown around a lot. Be very careful that you use it in context. You can either wipe people out with an unresolvable concept or you can give them a helpful message to process! Repent, from the original language, means "think again" or "think differently." There are two concepts from Scripture for repentance and conversion (Acts 3:19):

1. Think differently. Change your mind. Jesus challenged us to reset our thinking. "I believe in Christianity as I believe that the sun has risen: not only because I see it but because by it I see everything else." —C. S. Lewis. Always allow God to give you new insight and new perspectives. You see, repentance is less about sin and more about insight!

2. Realize that you are on the wrong path, ask for forgiveness, and simply make a decision to correct your course.

Don't view this repentance process as an inconvenience. Everyone wants quick results. But you need to understand that results are the final part of the process of repentance. It may take you a while to get results, but don't get discouraged by the length of time that it may take. Everyone is looking for significance, to feel special, and have a unique purpose which is the goal of the process. But 'significance' is different for each of us. It is all about your mindset. A change of mind will be a huge key in this process. You will know when you have completed the "repentance process" when your mind is changed.

It is during this repentance process that you will understand who you are. You will understand more about your calling. You will find balance in your daily life. You will discover your strong suits and figure out how to use them purposefully. If you simply view repentance as a constant correction for sinning, you will miss the deeper aspects of it. You will fail to see the opportunities! True repentance is a change of mind.

Allow the Holy Spirit to take you through the repentance process. "On the last and greatest day of the Feast, Jesus stood and said in a loud voice, "If anyone is thirsty, let him come to me and drink. Whoever believes in me, as the Scripture has said, streams of living water will flow from within him. By this He meant the Spirit, whom those who believed in Him were later to receive. Up to that time the Spirit had not been given, since Jesus had not yet been glorified." —John 7:37-39 (NIV).

Deeper than your sin, deeper than your emotions, deeper than your understanding, lives the Holy Spirit. He is resident in your "innermost" being. He dwells within you deeper than anything. He operates from the inside out. What an amazing opportunity! He is there to help you change your direction, and to think differently.

Head versus heart. People fall in one of two categories. Either they are led by their heart or they are led by their head. Either their emotions drive them or they follow their intellect and their limited understanding. But, honestly, to be balanced you can't really have one without the other. Your head needs to teach your heart. Your heart needs the balance of your intellect. They go hand-in-hand. Plutarch said, "The mind is not a vessel to be filled but a fire to be kindled." That is the balance!

As we continue to go through these six areas, you're going to find that they all really work together. A guitar has six strings, and for the music to sound full and complete, you need all six of them to be in tune. If one of the strings is out of tune, it affects the total sound. It's no longer pleasing. It's only when you bring that string back into tune that you have the tonal harmony. Likewise, your spiritual and emotional lives are interconnected. It's hard to separate one from the other. You are led by your ideals and your theories. But don't forget to be true in what you do. Don't allow your head to take over. It is your emotions, your heart, that balance your knowledge and your understanding. It's that balance that truly leads to wisdom.

Science, philosophy and faith. In the modern western world there seems to be quite a bit of confusion on these subjects. Many people think that science and faith aren't compatible. It seems to be an either/or situation. But this is certainly not the case. This misunderstanding is actually a lack of knowledge about the philosophy of science, which sees science and faith from different perspectives. At 21, understanding the nature of science, philosophy and faith will make things a whole lot easier for you in two areas:

1. **Love God with your mind.** (Mark 12:30). Being a Christian and an intellectual at the same time is most certainly possible. Do not bury your doubt, but confront it instead. Take the questions you have seriously.

2. **Dialogue with skeptics.** (Acts 18:4). Many people will dialogue with you about Christianity's reliability. Some of them will confrontationally call you an idiot while others are honestly seeking answers to their questions. They all want to know whether Christianity makes sense intellectually. Be prepared when that happens.

Has science disproved God? Science can tell us quite a bit about how the world works. We understand a lot about the universe thanks to the hard work of some great minds. But we still understand such a small percentage of the whole. Each day we discover and understand more. Does this mean that our capacity for God becomes smaller and smaller? Only if you believe in the "God of the gaps," meaning we stuff God into all the things we don't understand. Stay with me here. As we continue to learn, the room for God becomes smaller and smaller. We conclude that God is a hypothesis that we don't need anymore. But the biblical description of God is nothing like that. God is described as the creator. For example, He created gravity. He's not described as the one constantly pushing everything to the ground. The Bible describes Him as the writer of the laws governing the universe, and the creator of space, time, and matter. God is the creator of science.

God and modern physics. Interesting discoveries in physics have been made during our lifetime, one of them being the Big Bang Theory (1965). Before the evidence supporting that particular theory was discovered, it was troubling for Christians to defend Creation. Physicists widely agreed that the universe was static (infinite and unchanging). But the discovery of the expanding universe changed that perception. (Isaiah 44:24, Jeremiah 10:12) The expanding universe concept makes it possible for Christian's to defend Creation with confidence.

The philosophy of science. Nothing in the world of science disproves God. That is a fact. To speak of such things from a scientific perspective you have to make an interpretation of the scientific data available, then it becomes a matter of philosophy. Einstein said that "… the man of science is a poor philosopher." Science is amazing! It's a great source for knowledge. But when we use science to speak about God, we must move beyond the scientific scope. We must move into the area of philosophy (metaphysics). At this point, it isn't just about science. It's about understanding the science from a larger point of view. It's very important to understand the difference between science, the available information, and what we interpret from the information.

God and philosophy. Many thoughtful arguments have been made about God since ancient Greece (possibly even before then). Some of them are still highly relevant and widely discussed. Stuff like "the cosmological argument", "the moral argument", and "the teleological argument" are interesting to study, and can help people who have questions about God's existence. But they can only take you so far, as they are concepts and not evidence. They do not provide proof of Gods existence. They serve well to provoke thoughtful debate with skeptics, but it's rarely enough to lead someone to Christ.

Is faith blind? Do you really have to put your trust in something, no matter what the evidence points toward? Not at all! No matter what you believe in; atheism, theism, deism, pantheism, or even "heavy metalism," you are a person of faith. The truth is that what we can know beyond a shadow of a doubt turns out to be very little! Seriously! For example, the inevitability or unquestionable fact that 1+1=2, the whole is greater than part of the whole, or that I exist. When considering your worldview intellectually, look for things you can know "beyond *reasonable* doubt." So, where do we then go from here? How can we trust our worldview? The best way to define faith intellectually is by the concept of "*Inference to the best explanation*" (Abduction). This means that you look at all the data available, and then look at how it can best be explained. In your case, you want to establish your worldview. To do so, you will need to look at all the things you know about science, history, theology, philosophy, etc. But is that enough? Well, no. Finding truth is also an emotional experience. Your faith needs to be reasonable, but it shouldn't be ignorant. Remember that your heart always needs to balance your mind. Ask difficult questions. Don't be afraid of them. Remember that the Holy Spirit inside of you—who primarily works through your emotions—will guide you to truth!

Christianity's power to explain. Christianity is the only worldview that makes sense of the origin of the universe, the laws of nature, the fine-tuning of the universe, trusting our mental faculties (epistemology), and the resurrection of Christ. The amazing thing is that Christianity can be tested as well. In your walk with the Lord, you will experience things that cannot be explained by other worldview's. When you allow the Holy Spirit to work inside of you, you will have a worldview that you can trust beyond all reasonable doubt. So don't be discouraged when you find yourself in doubt. Take the questions you have seriously and continue to let the Holy Spirit work inside of you!

Few these days would argue that Jesus existed, but is He God? People during His time on earth were not only aware of His death on the cross, but they also witnessed His resurrection. They couldn't argue with the fact that Jesus had come back to life. He walked among them for 40 days before He ascended into Heaven. They simply didn't know what to do with Him. They didn't know how to explain Him. Many didn't want to explain Him. The religious leaders were busy doing damage control. Jesus had forced them to not only talk about Him, but to make a conclusion based on the events surrounding Him. We, as well, are forced to take a position on this subject. There is simply no escaping the question, "is He God?" Many called him a great teacher, but didn't believe his claims to be God. But does that even make sense?

> "I am trying here to prevent anyone saying the really foolish thing that people often say about Him: I'm ready to accept Jesus as a great moral teacher, but I don't accept his claim to be God. That is the one thing we must not say. A man who was merely a man and said the sort of things Jesus said would not be a great moral teacher. He would either be a lunatic—on the level with the man who says he is a poached egg—or else he would be the Devil of Hell. You must make your choice. Either this man was, and is, the Son of God, or else a madman or something worse. You can shut him up for a fool, you can spit at him and kill him as a demon or you can fall at his feet and call him Lord and God, but let us not come with any patronizing nonsense about his being a great human teacher. He has not left that open to us. He did not intend to."
>
> **C.S. LEWIS, *MERE CHRISTIANITY***

It's impossible to have a relationship with the "historical" Jesus. To many, He was just a figure in our history. Trying to establish a relationship with a public figure is like trying to connect with Abraham Lincoln. I know he was a good guy, and he did some great things that I can emulate. But at the end of the day, he is still simply a part of history. And so it is with Jesus… until you make it personal. Why am I writing this to you, knowing that you are already a Christian? Because your tendency is to relate to Him historically and through His past teaching, which still makes Him simply a public figure, just like Lincoln. The point is this: He became personal when He died on the cross, and opened a way for honest communication. He established a connection. Unless you are very aware of that connection, you will not fully comprehend the tremendous gift you have been given. Until then, your concept of the Christian life can only be about discipline— trying to be the best you can be. But when you "connect," you take it a step further. You accept his work on the cross as "finished," and you begin your new walk with Him in the Spirit. You make the leap from your head to your heart.

Set your mind free! For some people, becoming a Christian results in bondage. It seems they give away their freedom to join some kind of cult. And Christianity can feel that way with a legalistic mindset. You need to remember that Jesus came to set you free. Don't allow those, in legalistic bondage to their faith, to influence you towards the same bondage.

Some non-Christians will accuse you of not being a freethinker simply because you are a Christian. To them, Christianity is based on a myth and every Christian is in bondage to religion. It's understandable why they may think this way. As I have said, many Christians are very much in bondage to their faith. Being a Christian does not mean you cannot be a freethinker. It is so important that people see the freedom in your life. Christian freedom is so misunderstood. Modern people view freedom as being unlimited. They don't want anyone to tell them what to do. But the reality is that our choices have consequences and we live with those consequences, good and bad. Christian freedom is about staying away from things that put you in bondage. And when you fail, God is still there to forgive and restore you. Grace gives us an opportunity to let go of the past and move forward.

"Whoever controls the media, controls the mind" (Jim Morrison).
There are so many messages being thrown at you from radio, television, newspapers, and movies. In the future you will be dealing with twitter, Instagram, Facebook, YouTube, whew! The list goes on and on. In our "politically correct" society, we have forgotten what morality is really all about. In fact, in my lifetime, I have seen moral issues go from extremely unacceptable to commonplace. Many of these issues have even been adopted into the Christian lifestyle, though many are actually contrary to Biblical teachings. How does that happen? It seems when we hear something often enough, we begin to adopt it—or lose our resolve to stand against it. This is one reason it is so important to make sure your heart is set on Godly things. The Bible needs to be your foundation for morality, and not the media, which is always changing. Even though "everyone else is doing it," you can't afford to take your focus off the things that are truly important!

Be careful of pride. It will raise its ugly head when you least expect it. And, it's easy to have false humility. It's easy to get "puffed up" over things that you accomplish, and forget that it's God's power and His wisdom that you are using anyway! But this takes time. It happens as you continue to walk with the Lord, and continue to experience His power in your life. You begin to realize how little you are capable of, and the magnitude of what He is doing inside of you. It will happen during those times when you become sufficiently confused. When you realize you can no longer push forward with your strength alone. When you must rely on His wisdom and His strength. It isn't about you; be careful you don't call attention to yourself. Pride brings with it an uncomfortable fall. Sometimes a very long uncomfortable fall.

Avoid the feeling of superiority over others. There are times when you feel like you can do things better, smarter, wiser, and more efficient than everyone else around you. While you may have talent in several areas, you will find you do NOT have talent in all areas. One of the biggest lessons you have yet to learn is how to work well with others. Your tendency is to do things on your own, and become a "Lone Ranger Christian." You almost believe you can do anything. You don't necessarily need people to help. You feel invincible. And you are so wrong. You will learn in the years to come just how vulnerable you are, and just how much you're still lacking. There is still much you don't know. And, once again, that is the reason you truly need people around you to complete you. You are not in this alone!

Stop being offended. Start engaging the world! More and more, it seems that Christians are isolating themselves from the rest of the world. They seem content living in their own bubbles, speculating and condemning the world from their safe zones. They seem surprised when the non-Christian world makes "wrong" decisions. They have an opinion on almost any subject, often without even hearing both sides of an issue. They post fiery comments on Facebook and throw their judgment all over the Internet. And they do all of this from within their little, safe, comfortable bubbles. Seriously?! Is this the kind of influence Jesus asked us to have in the world? You need to quit being offended! Instead, you must engage the world. The world doesn't need your judgment. It needs your love! It needs to see a real Christian living a real life. The good. The bad. The ugly!

It isn't US verses THEM! We are "THEM". We are all "THEM." There is only one category. Christians seem to think they are in some kind of exclusive club that makes them better than anyone else around them. They talk down to people who are not saved, or not attending the "right" church. And they continue to alienate people simply because of their superior attitude. As you fully comprehend what you have been saved FROM, you will become more and more humble. In yourself, you truly are filthy rags in the sight of God. There is no one that does "good"—not even one!

What do you believe? Is it really possible to know God? And if so, why do so many Christians have such confusing diversity? There are two ways to read the Bible:

1. Reading with your agenda, so you already have an idea of what you want it to say.

2. Reading without an agenda, so you can discover what it is actually saying.

Now I realize I am being very general here, and it isn't always this cut and dry. But to really get to the heart of who God is and experience His attributes in a very real way in your life, you need to leave your agenda behind. Establish a set of beliefs from the Bible that will define your faith. Theology is not a frightening thing. "Theo" = God. "ology" = the study of. "*The study of God.*" Sounds like a wonderful way to get to know Him, doesn't it? Studying the Bible isn't the only way to get to know God. Nature tells us a lot about our creator's creativity, intelligence, etc. This is called natural theology. We can also know God through experience. Our daily walk with God shows us a lot about who He is. But more importantly the Holy Spirit reveals truth inside of us. He guides us in the situations we face, and through that, we learn to separate right from wrong.

Your actions will always follow your beliefs. Many call themselves "Christians," but their actions seem to prove otherwise. When you question them about their faith, they will explain how there are so many with differing opinions, and it is just impossible to know the specifics, the truth. One person told me, "I don't like theology. I don't even like to read. I'm just in love with Jesus." I almost said, "Jesus who?" How can you be "in love" with someone you know nothing about? Now, there are different ways to gather information: through sermons, listening to God in prayer, etc. If your goal as a Christian is to become "Christ like," then you need to know everything you can about Christ! Otherwise you will end up creating a god in *your* image...

Don't use your beliefs to beat people over the head! Many people use knowledge for power. You probably know the kind of person I'm talking about. They are always looking for things to disagree with. They see themselves as "defenders of the faith." They are always correcting and challenging everyone. Even though it is important that each of us live our convictions, it is even more important that you allow those convictions to shine through you. Don't get so caught up that you are perceived as an uptight intellectual. For many, 'uptight intellectual' is another name for "bully." Instead, show your faith by letting it transform you and guide you every day. Share your knowledge with people in a gentle way. Be someone people enjoy conversing with about faith and the challenges that result from such conversation.

Don't be so busy defending the faith that you forget to enjoy it!
Jesus came to set you free. And He told us that He didn't want us to
get caught up again in a yoke of bondage. The best part about being a
Christian is your relationship with Him. From time to time you will
be called upon to defend the faith. And when you do, be wise. Share
your experiences from a heart of love. Since the Holy Spirit lives deep
inside of you, He will always work through your emotions and your
mind. Don't be so busy defending your faith that you forget to connect with Him. That is the most important thing. Besides, no one can
argue with your experience. If people can see how the Holy Spirit truly
changes your life, it becomes difficult for them to argue that Christianity isn't real.

Don't assume the answer to a crisis of faith is atheism. While it may seem at times that there are legitimate faith questions that cannot be answered, that is true with anything in life. You will always find difficult questions and concerns in any relationship—including your relationship with God. You will study looking for answers to your questions and come away with more questions. And that's a good thing! "Lean on, trust in, and be confident in the Lord with all your heart and mind and do not rely on your own insight or understanding. In all your ways know, recognize, and acknowledge Him, and He will direct and make straight and plain your paths."—Proverbs 3:5-6: 5 (AMP). Even though your enormous curiosity seems like a burden now, it will serve you well and it will bring you great joy. Christianity is a quest, an adventure, and there will always be more to learn. In time, you will make your peace with that. Your journey should always generate questions. Don't throw out 95% of your foundation simply because you can't answer 5% of your questions! Learn to celebrate the answers you have as your foundation because you have the mind of Christ! The Bible tells us to "let this mind be in you that is also in Christ Jesus." (Phil. 2:5) And then in 1 Cor. 2:16, we are told, "you have the mind of Christ!" This is the perfect foundation for your continuing quest. You have HIS mind to lead you! Don't be afraid to ask the difficult questions. You have the God of the universe inside of you. He has some pretty exciting answers, which you will discover on your journey.

God didn't promise you happiness. I often say that happiness is "the feeling you have between catastrophes!" Happiness doesn't last. It's based on your circumstances, and your current situation. Though you will find that it's always fleeting, do not be discouraged. Don't feel like there's something wrong with your faith or with you. Happiness is fleeting for everyone! The cool thing about being a Christian is that God gives us a new foundation. The fruit of the Spirit contains joy. And joy is lasting. The Bible says that we can feel peace in the middle of a storm. This means that the Holy Spirit who lives deep inside of us gives us His peace when we need it most. It tells us that joy knows no end. I have the verse from Nehemiah 8:10 tattooed on my arm in four different languages: "The joy of The Lord is my strength." These are things that we can feel no matter what the situation is, no matter what the circumstances are. They are not based on outward influence. They come from your innermost being. From that place where the Holy Spirit lives inside of you. So as happiness comes and goes, joy can be there constantly.

You can expect tragedy in your life. No one lives life without it. People around you will die. You will suffer loss personally, in your friendships and with your family. Sometimes life sucks, and isn't fair. Just about the time you think everything is going very well; your world can fall apart. It's during these times that you need to figure out how you're going to handle it. We've talked about fighting the battle before the battle. This is another one of those situations where this preparation will come in handy. Expect tragedy. It will come. And it will always happen when you least expect it. And, when it happens, you will either want to run to God, or run away from Him. You can raise your hand and ask Him to connect with you or you can raise your hand in a fist and blame Him for whatever happens. You can push Him away, or draw closer to Him. At times, it will seem aggravating and hopeless. You will find, as you mature in your faith, that the greatest place to be in the time of tragedy is in His arms. His comfort and His wisdom is very important to you during these times. But again, decide what you're going to do before tragedy strikes. Then, when it does, it's simply a matter of following the course you've already set.

SPIRITUAL

"Give up your good Christian life, and follow Jesus."
GARRISON LEILLOR

You don't have what it takes. Picture this: Here's a group of guys who followed Jesus around. They were His disciples. They learned from Him, both from their talks and by watching Him. They saw Him crucified. They spent more time with Him after He raised from the dead. And then they watched Him ascend into Heaven on a cloud. His final words to them, "go into all the world and share the Gospel" were specific. I can imagine they were ready to go! Most likely, they felt pumped and equipped. After all, they were His personal disciples. But… it wasn't enough. Jesus told them to go into the upper room to pray and wait. Seriously?! Wait? How?? Why??? He was so specific; go and share. He was so specific, pray and wait! Which is correct? Are you confused, well the answer is simple!!

The Answer is simple, but the process is not. Jesus knew they would never really succeed in their own strength. They needed to wait for the Holy Spirit. Until you have allowed the Holy Spirit to empower you from your innermost being, you are not ready either. There are so many around you who are simply teaching rules, principles, and ideals, but all without a heart and connection. Jesus knew the information itself wasn't enough. The disciples needed deeper wisdom and understanding that could only come from the Holy Spirit. So do you.

> *But the spiritual man tries all things [he examines, investigates, inquires into, questions, and discerns all things], yet is himself to be put on trial and judged by no one [he can read the meaning of everything, but no one can properly discern or appraise or get an insight into him].*

1 CORINTHIANS 2:15 AMP

Therefore, there is now no condemnation for those who are in Christ Jesus (Romans 8:1). It still confuses me how so many people are preaching condemnation when the Bible tells us that Jesus removed it through His death on the cross. Mis-practiced Christianity is offensive to people. They feel condemned and judged by the church. To believe that we have the moral high ground as Christians is truly sickening. Always remember, "there is now no condemnation for those who are in Christ Jesus!" You will do well personally and in your ministry to put this into perspective. Understand the difference and practice it. People desperately need to hear this message over and over again.

Living the Christian life is impossible. Yes, that's what I said. And you already know this to be true. Most pastors and teachers tell you how important it is to discipline yourself to not sin. You feel very guilty that you are failing to be perfect. You *are* failing. And you will continue to fail. God knows you are failing as well. If you were able to live the kind of life that is pleasing to God all on your own, Jesus' death on the cross would have been in vain. The Bible tells us that Jesus set us free from the law of sin and death. How did he do it? He forgave us. He took our sins away. Past. Present. Future. They were nailed to the cross. Forgiven. It has been done. Why don't we hear more about that? Why doesn't this news cause us extreme excitement every day we're alive? Why do we continue to talk so much about sin? The answer turns out to be quite simple; in the back of our minds we are still hoping that we will someday be good enough and disciplined enough to do all of this on our own. But it will never happen. And when you realize this, you will cling to what Jesus has done. The joy of realizing this is beyond words!

There is a huge difference between *discipline* and *surrender*. Discipline is a dead-end street. You will always be disappointed. You will always fall short. You will always sit in your own judgment. It's like putting all your energy into striving after success, but never moving forward. Since Jesus died on the cross, surrender is the course we follow. We are now asked to "believe" rather than discipline ourselves. In the original language of the Bible, "believe" from John 3:16 means, "to trust in, to rely on, to cling to". That's a bit different than trying to do it all on your own! Instead of being consistently frustrated by your inability to be good enough, you realize it has nothing to do with your abilities. It is the Holy Spirit working inside of you. He gives you these qualities as a result of His work in your innermost being. And by surrendering, you are giving up your agenda; you are letting the Holy Spirit do what He wants with you. And that sin that you are working so hard to get rid of? Well, it disappears faster, since HE is the one doing all the hard work. This might take some time, even years, to grasp. But trust me, it is worth it!

You will never have enough faith. In the back of your mind, you are waiting to become more spiritually clear minded. You look forward to that time when you get older and wiser. I am now 41 years older as I write to you. I am wiser in many areas. And I am more aware of my failings than I have ever been. I told you at the beginning of my letters that I am disappointed at the place where I am at today. I really had thought I would be further along in my spiritual life. But the realization that there is always something to learn is to my advantage. It keeps me connected and dependent on God. After all these years of studying the Bible, living the faith, experiencing God speaking to me and watching Him provide miracle after miracle, I am more aware of my lack of faith than ever before. I know that my ability to "have" faith doesn't depend on my power to produce it. But rather, the deeper faith that I so badly need comes from Him. I can feel it when He initiates it. I am more and more aware that I must continue to get out of His way and allow Him to fill me with belief. It's why the disciple said, "I believe, Lord. Help my unbelief." You would do well to change your approach on this subject. Instead of thinking that you are someday going to become the spiritual giant you envisioned in your mind, realize that He is your source. Allow Him to move in you. Allow Him to give you more faith when your faith fails you. Then, you will find yourself going above and beyond your expectations. Instead of you setting the bar, He sets it, and higher than you could ever envision.

It's okay to get angry with God. His desire is for you to share all of your emotions with Him; including your misunderstandings. Never worry about offending Him. God wants you to bring everything before Him, even the anger and frustration you might feel towards Him. He's big enough, and I promise you He can take it! God already knows everything that is going on inside of you. So the reason for sharing your feelings with Him is so *you* become aware of everything going on inside you! Communicating your feelings with God requires you to figure out what to communicate and then express it. God understands so much more than you can imagine. Just let Him know when you're confused by what He is doing. Those honest and deep conversations are of great value. In time you will appreciate those moments more and more.

Are you having difficulty finding God when you are in pain? I am sure you are… you and every other Christian in the world! It's difficult to hear His voice when you are frustrated and emotionally driven. You feel overwhelmed with the enormity of your problems and your feelings. So you ask for help. Christian friends say, "Well, God has a plan. You just have to trust that He knows what He is doing. Look at Job." Ouch! Not exactly what you wanted to hear! Not only do you feel even worse, you also feel even more alone with your problems. You will find that many Christian friends are ready to give you a ready-made-and-rehearsed-beforehand answer to those complex challenges in life—as if they have never gone through anything like this! "You just have to have faith. Just pray it through." Ouch again! Seriously?! The Bible tells us to "rejoice with those who rejoice; mourn with those who mourn" (Romans 12:15 NIV). Again, it is all about compassion and unconditional love. It is about putting yourself in others shoes and identifying with them. You have to understand this concept, or well-meaning people will simply add to your confusion and pain. AND, you need to remember this when others look to you for guidance when they are searching for God in their pain. Make sure you surround yourself with people who are willing to both rejoice and mourn with you. You will absolutely need their help when difficult times come.

Relationships. The foundation for all of your relationships should be honesty. Pursuing each other, pursuing God, and getting to know yourself. If these pursuits aren't based on honesty and trust, then you've missed the most important detail. Continue to seek a personal relationship with God. Always remember that Christianity is about a relationship and not a religion. I wish you would have known more about this at 21. At this point, you believe the more you study and prepare, the better Christian you will become. Although study in the Word of God gives you a better picture of who God is, it's not a substitute for a relationship with Him.

There are a lot of belief systems out there. There are systems for religion, even systems for faith. People pursue faith many ways.

1. **Faith in your belief system.** Many people don't get any farther than this. They have faith in the system. They study. They examine. They memorize. They force themselves to read the scripture. But it stops there.

2. **Faith in your faith.** Many Christians get caught up in this thinking, without even realizing what they're doing. They name it and claim it in Jesus name. They have faith in their faith, but they walk blindly. There's no substance. Without realizing it, you are falling into this trap. It's more important that you understand the heart of God and the heart of ministry, than to commit yourself to doctrinal stubbornness.

3. **Faith in the object of your faith.** And of course, the object of your faith is Jesus Christ. This is where it begins and this is where it ends. This is the one that works.

Be careful how you define your faith. There are many who define their faith by saying, "I believe in the kind of God that…" What a frightening way to live! At 21, you are doing a lot of that. You put God in your own box. You believe in a few things that aren't necessarily true. Let God define Himself! Don't make the mistake of saying, "if I just had more faith, I'd be a better Christian." That isn't true either. It isn't a matter of having more faith, but rather, a matter of having a closer relationship with Jesus Christ.

Silence can be your greatest blessing. Again, this is one of the things you struggle with the most. You fall asleep to the radio or to music, since silence causes you to think about issues you are trying to forget. Silence for you is uncomfortable and lonely. It even feels painful sometimes. But the lack of silence keeps you from a deeper relationship with God. You will find as you get older that His "still small voice" will become the most important voice in your life. And those times that you are in silence will become time for correction, examination, creativity, and planning. God will inspire you when you take the time to be quiet and listen to Him. Prayer becomes more meaningful and powerful when you understand the key ingredients. "And when you pray, you must not be like the hypocrites. For they love to stand and pray in the synagogues and at the street corners, that they may be seen by others. Truly, I say to you, they have received their reward. But when you pray, go into your room and shut the door and pray to your Father who is in secret. And your Father who sees in secret will reward you. And when you pray, do not heap up empty phrases as the Gentiles do, for they think that they will be heard for their many words. Do not be like them, for your Father knows what you need before you ask him." (Matthew 6:5 ESV).

Learn to have meaningful conversations with God and with yourself. This is uncomfortable for you right now. You feel a lack of control with this kind of depth. But again, there is a good reason for your discomfort. Prayer really involves more listening than talking. It involves intimacy (Into-me-see) with ourselves and then with God. Your biggest problem at this point in your life is that you are not having meaningful conversations with God. Your motivation comes mostly from wanting to do the right things, and your desire to lead others to do the same. But there is still that deep longing inside of you that desperately needs to connect with God in a much deeper way. And your deeper loneliness is only more profound in silence. So your prayers are much more general and undefined. They are more agenda driven. It is difficult for you to really discern the heart of God and His desires for you. You are listening, but not very well. Be quiet. Process in silence. Learn in silence. Take everything to your "quiet place". Think and pray it through. This will become your greatest strength.

Dietrich Bonhoeffer is a hero to me. So wise and yet so down-to-earth. You will learn a lot about silence and prayer from him. "*The Christian needs to be alone during a definite period of each day for meditation on scripture…and for prayer…even during times of spiritual dryness and apathy.*" Powerful suggestion! But the principle that has changed my life more profoundly is his teaching on how to pray for others: "*I move into the other man's place. I enter his life…his guilt and distress. I am afflicted by his sins and his infirmity.*" When praying for others, you need to know how it feels to walk in their shoes. You need to imagine how it feels to be them, so you can feel empathy for them instead of condemnation. It is this intimacy in prayer for others that will profoundly change your life and your perspectives.

Your past is passed. You've made some mistakes. You've learned some lessons. Now move on. Don't waste your time with remorse. Use what you've learned as a basis for future decisions. When we were younger, our father told the story about a man who worked in a bank. During the course of the man's day, he realized that he had made a million dollar mistake. There was nothing he could do. It was too late. His mistake was about to cost the bank $1 million, and it was his fault. So, he prepared his letter of resignation, and went into the bank presidents' office. He laid his letter of resignation on the desk, and said, "I've just made a million dollar mistake that cannot be reversed. I'm very sorry. Here is my letter of resignation." The banks president looked at the letter and looked at him, and asked him to sit down. After what seemed like an eternity, he spoke. "I'm not happy with what you have done, but I have decided not to terminate you. There's one thing I know for sure. You are the one person in this bank that will never make this mistake again. Let's turn this into a million-dollar lesson." We all have million-dollar lessons. It truly sucks to have made those mistakes, but we cannot change them. The important thing is that we use them for the future. We're more equipped than ever when we learn from our mistakes and can move past them focusing on the present and the future.

Sadly, you don't have an erase button. You will always remember many shortcomings and mistakes that you'd like to forget; memories of failures, memories of lost love. Memories of… coulda, shoulda, woulda. Along with those memories, you'll have that miserable feeling in the pit of your stomach that will never go away. But, there is a silver lining! Every failure becomes an opportunity. You can never go back and redo those things, but you can make different choices in the future. Don't waste your time in remorse. Move on. Move ahead. Move forward.

Don't define yourself by your past. It is so easy to personalize your defeats. So many people around you have suffered great abuse. Child molestation. Rape. Debilitating illness. And many times they get stuck there. They can't move on. When you ask them to define who they are, they make comments like, "I'm a rape victim." "I suffered severe injuries in a car accident." "I grew up in a home with an alcoholic father." These things are indeed horrible. No one should have to suffer these kinds of abuses. But many people get stuck there, sometimes for the rest of their lives. That's the wonderful thing about becoming a Christian. God gives us a fresh start! "Therefore if any man be in Christ, he is a new creature: old things are passed away; behold, all things are become new." (2 Corinthians 5:17 ESV). I don't want to oversimplify this! Getting past a tragic experience is a difficult and long process. But once you grasp that it doesn't define you, you take a major step in the right direction. You then have the foundation you need to move on.

Remember that God loves you because of who He is. It has nothing to do with anything you do, or fail to do. It isn't earned and it has nothing to do with how you perform. It's His unconditional gift to you. Accept it, and be blessed by it. Remind yourself about it when you mess up. Don't forget about it when you don't feel loved. That blessing will carry you father than you can possibly imagine!

Be aware of the Holy Spirit's signals. Just as your body will send you signals: Tired, happy, hungry, sad, etc. The Holy Spirit does the same thing. This does not only happen from your innermost being, but it also happens through the Body of Christ around you—the church family. The Holy Spirit speaks to you through your Christian brothers and sisters. Remember to listen. For you, listening to your physical body is an area needing improvement. God created your body and designed the Holy Spirit's ability to communicate with you. Both will get your attention if you allow them to. Take them both seriously.

The Holy Spirit is more than a circus act. So many are wondering where they can go to see the Holy Spirit perform. The local church marque reads, "Holy Spirit Revival Here Friday at 7:00 PM." A more honest sign would read, "Show up on Friday and we'll have the Holy Spirit perform for you, with a lot of signs and wonders." And how do they know how the Holy Spirit will move, and at what time and which day it will happen? So many in the Christian community have reduced the Holy Spirit to a carnival event. He is not there to perform, but rather, to transform. If your idea of His purpose is simply to show you a bunch of cheap tricks, then you will miss the deeper transformation that He came to perform inside of you. Be careful. Keep your focus on His purpose. "But the Helper, the Holy Spirit, whom the Father will send in My name, He will teach you all things, and bring to your remembrance all things that I said to you." (John 14:26 ESV)

Not everything has to fit into a system. Often we find it easier to follow a system. Many people just want a list to follow, they just want to hear what to believe and then believe it. But this is not the way God works. A good leader or mentor will show you and/or tell you how to find your own answers instead of just telling you what to believe. A good leader is a servant who leads others to think for themselves. They lead by walking with you, not ahead of you—and not behind you! The best answers are the honest ones. "How did God lead you?" No hype. Just complete honesty. The Holy Spirit is your driving force. The Holy Spirit instructs, and those around you should nurture.

Stop reading the Bible! You've spent many years studying and forcing yourself to read the bible every day. Now stop. There's a huge difference between studying the Bible and falling in love with its author. All the study and memorization in the world won't lead you to a personal relationship. Remember that study is for one purpose: To fall in love with God and to learn more about him!

Pick up the Bible again. This time, begin reading it from your heart. I repeat. Instead of adopting a disciplined daily reading schedule, begin to read from your heart. Get to know the author. Read even if it's just a few sentences every day. Make your pursuit to really understand His heart. Read the Bible with your heart and not just out of obligation. Reading the Bible, prayer, spending time with other believers… all of these "disciplines" lead to freedom once you have established a heart for God. You will find new meaning and new enthusiasm when it comes from your heart instead of a sense of obligation.

Legalism will burn you out. When we adopt a checklist and a set of rules to live by, we have forgotten that there is something much more important: GRACE! It is the very thing that Jesus was trying to get across to us when He asked us to avoid becoming like the Pharisees. Agapé love separates legalism from grace. Operating in grace gives us more energy. Legalism wipes us out!

Quit forcing yourself to live the Christian life. As long as you are forcing yourself to live the Christian life by following a prescribed set of standards… daily Bible reading, witnessing, church attendance, etc… you will create a foundation for religion, and lose focus for the real foundation; your intimate relationship with Christ. Without focus on the right foundation, your efforts will create burn-out in your spiritual life and interrupt your passion and heart for God. For instance, if you were to read a book about friendship, you may have knowledge about how to develop a friendship. But that book and your interpretation of its information is one sided. Relationships are at least two sided. You can only develop a relationship with someone by interacting with him or her. And this is true for your relationship with God. Reading the Bible daily, attending church, and interacting with others—though good for your Christian balance—will never take the place of intimacy with God.

When you interact with God, He is clear about what He is saying. We have to get out of the way and listen to what He's saying. He tells us the greatest commandment is Love. The greatest commandment is NOT to live a Christian life by modern church standards. He teaches us to have unconditional love. For God. For Others. For Yourself. Nothing else will make a significant impact in your personal life and your ministry. Your passion for God will only come from falling in love with him. Period.

The world today is a playground for extroverts. It seems the people who speak the loudest are the ones who are heard the most. At 21, you are one of them. You need to be seen. You need to be noticed. You continue to come up with compelling models on how to live your life and recommend others to do the same. It all sounds wonderful, but much of it is lacking in depth and personal intimacy. You still have so much to learn, but you are not very teachable in this area. Many of the people around you, whom you assume are weak and unmotivated, will actually prove to have some of the deepest resources for change in your life. Don't ignore them, and don't miss it! Remember the great benefit silence can have in your life.

The Gospel is not a gimmick! Many in the Christian faith have reduced it to that. They use the same advertising and sales schemes that we see being used to sell used cars on television. They speak as if Jesus is a commodity. They run attendance contests and advertise their churches as "the best," "better than the others," "more hip and on the edge," and "more spiritual and closer to God." I know if most of them could leave the mentality they are absorbed in, and take a look at the bigger picture, they would do things differently. Meanwhile, the world watches the Christian community market Jesus, and wonders why they use all this hype. To the average person, it seems dishonest and impersonal. And, at 21, you are dangerously close to doing the same thing. You keep looking for slick ways to present the Gospel through music. You are careful that your hair and dress are "hip" and current. Even though you pride yourself as being honest and engaging, there are times when you cross this line. Be careful. Jesus isn't a commodity. If you present Him this way, you may lead people past the point of what a personal relationship with Him is all about. If God has placed them in your path, then you should point them in the right direction.

Live your life in front of people! People will pay much more attention to how you live than what you say. 1 Peter 3:15 (PHILLIPS) says, "Be ready at any time to give a quiet and reverent answer to anyone who asks about the hope you have within you." One of the biggest obstacles for people to overcome as they try to find God is other Christians. Seriously?! Someone watching Christians live their lives could easily conclude that most Christians aren't any more "put together" than non-Christians! Christianity doesn't appear inviting. Many Christian lives reflect hate and oppression; where is the love? If someone can't see that Jesus makes a difference in your life, then they conclude that He isn't the truth. Make sure that you don't become one of those who have a belief system without a life-changing relationship with Jesus Christ. Allow people to see that Jesus is transforming you. Live your life in front of people. That's the greatest testimony you can give!

Continue to live outside of the box. But as you do, realize there are three things that are important.

1. You need a support system. Your family with their unconditional love and support has always paved a way for that to happen. Besides the support from family, make sure you also allow those who believe in you and know you to have a voice in your life.

2. Because of your extreme creativity, you need an outlet. You will always need to take a different road. But make sure that road is solid. Make sure it captures your spiritual and emotional interests. Make sure it becomes your "hill to die upon."

3. Be sure your walk with the Lord is solid. Your actual walk with the Lord and the strength of your personal relationship with Him is theologically conservative. Stay on that path. It is an excellent foundation to push outside the box, while allowing you the safeguards of God's Word and His ultimate purpose for your life.

There are challenges living outside of the box. I appreciate the fact that you don't have a need to be the same or do the same things as others around you. You will always hear "a different drummer." That will continue to be an adventure for you, but it will make life a bit confusing at times. While most people find it important to define their lives with a structure or plan, you have chosen a life of faith… **defining things** as you go. Some common defining structures include: a college education, a secure job, marriage, a house, a family, a dog, a car, retirement fund, etc. None of these things are very important to you at 21. But that doesn't mean they aren't important. I would caution you not to get so caught up living on the edge that you forget to take care of yourself. Even living outside of the box, you still need a box "home" to come back to from time to time. Don't segregate yourself from things that are important aspects of life itself simply because you are so focused on the edge. Get used to pausing from time to time and seeing the bigger picture. I love the fact that you live your life in wonder and follow after your passions. As long as the Holy Spirit is leading you, He will always make a way for you.

Remember that others are watching you. Does that mean that you need to be on your best behavior and remember to smile a lot? At 21 that is your thinking. You want to be able to model your faith in Jesus in a very positive way. And as a result, you stuff a lot of feelings, and hid your real life from others. The biggest challenge ahead of you is to be completely transparent and honest. And the only way you will accomplish this is to understand modeling your "best" behavior is not completely honest. Modeling every behavior is honest. You will come to understand that people need to see a real faith. They need to watch you succeed and fail. That's what real people do. No one is looking for perfection. They're looking for solutions. Therefore, it is more important that you show them your failures and your dependence on Christ to get back up, than an unrealistic religious experience that has no bearing in real life. It is exhausting to be so careful of what people see. It is liberating to simply follow Christ to the best of your abilities. "Follow my example, as I follow the example of Christ." (1 Corinthians 11:1 NIV)

Practice random acts of kindness. You are just beginning to learn how important it is to bless those around you. Just a simple word to a stranger will sometimes change the course of their whole day. Telling a good friend how much they mean to you can strengthen your friendship. Simply pausing throughout the day to give someone a word of encouragement can make a world of difference in their life. Practice giving things away—you don't really need as much stuff as you think. There are people around you in need, perhaps more needy than you. Give. Share. Downsize and give to those in need. You will bless others, and you'll find yourself living a happier life and feeling more fulfilled as a result.

You need to fight your addictions. What addictions? All of them. The ones you've had, the ones you have, and the ones that are possibilities for your future. Until now, you have not touched alcohol. Don't get started. You have not tried drugs. Again, don't get started. You have not looked at porn. Don't get started. Your tendency is to become addicted to things. You are an extreme person. It isn't just a matter of making "religious" decisions, but rather "wise" decisions. You know your own weaknesses. There are so many around you fighting all kinds of addictions. Most of them never dreamed they wouldn't be able to handle them. Their addictions surprise them. Don't be naive. You know better. Fight the battle before the battle. Simply don't get started. That continues to be the easiest way to fight addictions!

Stuff happens. Some temptations are actually overwhelming! You have this feeling that you are always in control, and will continue to be control. That is not true. You will encounter times when you simply don't feel like you can handle it. The Scriptures are full of people who felt overwhelmed. Some took their own lives, some became drunk, others "dropped out and ran". Why do these things happen? Didn't God promise that He wouldn't give us more than we can handle? "No temptation has overtaken you except what is common to mankind. And God is faithful. He will not let you be tempted beyond what you can bear. But when you are tempted, He will also provide a way out so that you can endure it." (1 Corinthians 10:13 NIV) There are three important points from this verse that you need to bear in mind:

1. **Your temptation is common**. When you go through temptation, you are not experiencing something that is unique just to you! It is quite simply a part of life. James 2–4 (NIV) says, "Consider it pure joy, my brothers and sisters, whenever you face trials of many kinds, because you know that the testing of your faith produces perseverance. Let perseverance finish its work so that you may be mature and complete, not lacking anything." You always feel quite alone when temptation strikes. And most of the time you feel that you can't talk to anyone about it, because they wouldn't understand. You would be surprised how many others are going through the same things! Share and ask for help. James 5 (NIV) says, "If any of you lacks wisdom, you should ask God, who gives generously to all without finding fault, and it will be given to you."

2. **God is faithful.** He won't allow you to be tempted beyond what you can bear. What? Didn't I just say that some temptations are overwhelming? Don't some temptations

actually result in suicide for some people? Even for Christians? Yes. But don't miss the point here. We can surely feel tempted beyond what we can bear. That is the whole reason God provides a way out so you can endure it. There has to be a time during your temptation when you turn it over to God and begin to use HIS strength and HIS power. James 1: 13-15 (NIV) says, "When tempted, no one should say, 'God is tempting me.' For God cannot be tempted by evil, nor does he tempt anyone; but each person is tempted when they are dragged away by their own evil desire and enticed. Then, after desire has conceived, it gives birth to sin; and sin, when it is full-grown, gives birth to death."

3. **Don't be angry with God.** This is the point when it is easy to question God about His love and His safety for you. It is easy to feel abandoned and alone during difficulties. But remember God promised, "he will never leave you or abandon you." (Deuteronomy 31:6 NIV) Instead of questioning God's faithfulness, decide to immediately rely on Him in your situation. You see, the secret to your endurance is to run TO God and not away from Him. Then, and only then, will you be able to endure it!

There are also those situations you put yourself into. It is very easy to set yourself up to be tempted before you have an opportunity to think it all through. Everything happens quickly, and not long afterwards, you find yourself drowning in a sea of temptation. It is easy to beat yourself up when you realize what you have done, and assume that since you got yourself into this mess, you can't ask God to get you out of it. BUT God is bigger than all of that. The Bible says it was "while we were yet sinners that Christ died for us." (Romans 5:8) Whatever the temptation, whether it was self-imposed or not, you can always count on God in His compassion to make a way for you!

You are not a failure. "I should have had more faith." "I should have believed God more." "I should have…" Seriously?! God knows all about your limited abilities. Again, God knows that you will never have enough faith. And instead of playing the "I should have" game, realize that you will always fall short in your faith. That is because it isn't a solitary effort but a partnership. Jesus promises to walk beside you. Working together. Guiding you all along the way. Instead of feeling remorse for your lack of faith, remind yourself of the real problem. You need to walk in harmony. Otherwise, you will keep playing the "should have" games in your head!

Don't be afraid of crisis. It is usually difficult times that bring you closer to God. Remember that God doesn't have any grandchildren. He only has sons and daughters. You can't rely on mom and dad's faith, or our grandparent's faith. It all comes down to your personal faith. And getting to that will most likely involve some difficult times. Don't be afraid of crisis. Don't be afraid to ask difficult questions. Don't simply believe something because everyone else does. God is faithful. He says, "...seek and you will find; knock, and the door will be opened to you. For everyone who asks receives, and the one who seeks finds, and to the one who knocks it will be opened." (Matthew 7:7-8 ESV) God isn't afraid to show himself to you if you seek Him where He may be found. "I believe, Lord. Help my unbelief" (Mark 9:24 ESV).

Compassion and love need to be the foundation for everything you do. It is so easy to get caught up in organizing, pioneering, and administrating—causing you to forget about the heart of things. This is your struggle at 21. You have a lot of great ideas. And you are working hard to make them happen. You see many needs in the body of Christ, and you continue to address them. Your passion is thinking outside the box. It always will be. You are aware of your capacity to make mistakes. You have already made many of them! There are times when it is difficult for you to separate your ideas from your God-given passions. You just keep building your empire without really stopping to evaluate where God is in all of your building or if He is even 'in' the building of the empire. At times, His voice seems difficult to hear. That is where compassion enters. Everything you do should be motivated by your compassion for people. And, again, that compassion comes from Him. Compassion must be at the very heart of your efforts. When you have that, you have everything. Your ability to discern the leading of the Holy Spirit in ministry becomes a lot easier. Instead of inviting people to be involved in the ministry, you invite them to become part of a very real family where they will feel valued, loved, and nurtured.

Choose encouragement rather than judgment when dealing with people. The church is usually quick to judge. It sees the sins of others, and wastes no time pointing them out. But Christ set a different example. He encouraged us. Even though He knew our shortcomings, He encouraged us anyway. He took simple fishermen and believed in them. He knew what they could become. What a wonderful example for you to follow as you work with people. Many times, because your emotions are involved, you will want to lash out in judgment at others. Be careful. Using encouragement rather than judgment is the biblical choice.

Be sure to use your spiritual gifts in the body of Christ. Church has become more of a spectator sport and less of a community of engaged believers. It seems that the spiritual gifts that should be used together in the body of Christ are left dormant. What a sad situation. No Pastor possesses all the spiritual gifts. Pastors will always be unbalanced in at least one area of their life. For a Pastor to be balanced, they need to receive from other people in the congregation. So remember you are not God's gift to the congregation or to the people around you. You will always be lacking in certain areas of your life. You have a lot to learn and that will always be true. You will always need the body of Christ to be complete.

> [Note: There are many spiritual gifts assessment questionnaires on the internet that can help you determine what your specific gifts are. Google it, and start using them!]

Son, brother, father. Those are the spiritual transitions that we go through as a Christian. You'll start out as a son. You are new in the faith. Your walk with Jesus is just getting started. Then, rather quickly, you'll become a brother. You realize there are others around you that are just like you. You have a lot of things in common. You continue to be a son, but you enjoy the brotherhood of other Christians. One day, you become a father. You realize you're a little older. You realize you have a little more responsibility. And you begin to mentor and father those who are younger. Enjoy and embrace these different seasons of your Christian life. Every one of them is a blessing. But take them very seriously. The depth of your relationship with God and with people will be directly related to where you are in your faith journey. The Bible says that the older men should teach the younger men. The older women should teach the younger women. It's wonderful when you get to that place. Look forward to it. It will happen sooner than you think!

Mentor someone. Ask God to lead you to those who have the same heart that you do. At this point in my life, I can honestly say my life would be seriously incomplete without those who have become "sons." It has been one of the unexpected joys of my life that make my life fuller than I could have imagined! It's also been a two-way street. I have honestly learned as much from them as they have from me. And mentoring others inspires me to push ahead and continue to learn and grow.

God's will in a nutshell... "Be joyful always; pray continually; give thanks in all circumstances, for this is God's will for you in Christ Jesus." (1 Thessalonians 5:16-18). Pretty simple and straight forward. Three short verses that pack a punch! Once you become a Christian and have the Holy Spirit working deep inside of you, some very powerful things become possible. View them as a circle. Be joyful. Pray Continually. Give thanks. There are a few things that are unique with this passage of Scripture:

1. Joy is not dependent on your ability to produce it, nor is it based on happiness. It is a fruit of the Holy Spirit who lives inside of you. It really has nothing to do with your outward circumstances, nor your capacity to control them. Joy is not fleeting. Because it is a fruit of the Spirit, it is there all the time. Of course there are times when you feel outside circumstances more than your inner joy, but that leads us to the next point.

2. Pray. All the time. That doesn't mean that you pray as if you are writing a letter. "Dear God, blah blah blah. Sincerely, Bob (amen)." Praying continuously involves your constant communication with the Holy Spirit inside of you. And that leads us to the next point...

3. Give thanks. In every circumstance. Notice it doesn't say "for" every circumstance. No matter what happens around you, the Holy Spirit inside of you produces His peace... and His joy. And there we are again. Full circle.

When you understand this, you have the perfect foundation for God to build upon. "For I can do everything through Christ, who gives me strength." (Philippians 4:13 NLT)

Most people have a "cosmic" picture of the Holy Spirit. They see Him as some mystical intangible being that remains impersonal. The Bible gives us three important foundations for our understanding of him.

1. **He has a location.** He lives in your inmost being.

2. **He has a purpose.** He is there to guide you into all truth and wisdom.

3. **He has a personality.** The Bible lists His emotional attributes: Love, joy peace, patience, kindness, goodness, faithfulness, gentleness, and self-control.

As you can see, His mission is defined, and His foundations are concrete. And because this is true we have His wisdom and His patterns to follow. "Do not conform any longer to the pattern of this world. But be transformed by the renewing of your mind. Then you will be able to test and approve what God's will is, His good, pleasing and perfect will." (Romans 12:2 NIV) So, with the Holy Spirit as your guide, you have what it takes to tackle any situation that comes along!

PHYSICAL

"Our own physical body possesses a wisdom which we who inhabit the body lack. We give it orders which make no sense."
HENRY MILLER

Eat, drink, sleep and get moving! This advice is boring to you and you certainly do not understand the importance of these things at this point in your life. I sure wish you did! Action at 21 would certainly save me from reaction at 62. The physical difficulties I experience now are because you consider this advice far down on the list of priorities. At 21, you have this feeling that you can do anything to your body and you will not suffer any negative consequences. Death and old age seem so far away, and because of this, you are not proactive with your body for the future. This concept of being invincible is so common at your age. But the fact that it is common does not make it right. You will find that 41 years will go by in the blink of an eye, and your body will reflect the results of your apathy.

While it is true that right now you can eat and drink anything you want and not feel any serious effects from it, you cannot do that forever. It will catch up with you. Eating healthy and hydrating daily will serve you well. You can find nutritional alternatives for almost any kind of food. Your body needs good fuel to run efficiently. I really wish I would have known that at 21. Here are some basic guidelines:

1. Eat Fresh. Choose fresh, natural foods over processed foods as much as possible.

2. Limit those things your body has trouble processing efficiently, like sugar, trans fats, too much wheat, etc. Eat organic produce and range fed meats as much as possible.

3. Eat in moderation. You don't need mass quantities of food. Your stomach isn't that big!

4. Drink a lot of pure water. Avoid sodas and sugar/chemical drinks.

5. Eat 6 small meals per day instead of 3 major ones. Allow your body to spread out the process of digestion throughout the day.

Sleep is a MAJOR issue. You may feel you can get away with 4 to 6 hours of sleep at night now, but this practice will catch up with you. God designed our bodies to get on the average of 8.5 hours of sleep per night. That is how long it takes to run through all of your sleep cycles. For some it is as little as 7.5, while others need 9, or even 10 hours. Find out what is right for you by falling asleep at the same time every night, and see what time you wake up feeling rested. Anything less leaves you lacking and will catch up with you in the long run. A lack of sleep will mess with your moods, energy, and stress level. It will even cause you to gain weight, and will increase your risk of disease. Don't take this lightly. It will absolutely have a profound effect on your life in the future.

Move! You don't have to wipe yourself out at the gym to be healthy. Walking every day is a good place to start. Studies show that even this can keep you fit and your body running in top condition. And again, everyone is different. Keeping your body happy through movement can include riding a bike to school or work every day or enjoying a brisk run through the park or heading to the gym and lifting weights. Whatever you do, make sure that you do something you enjoy. Otherwise, it will be short lived, and your health will pay for it in the long run.

Again, I realize this all sounds a bit boring, and unimportant. Especially when everyone around you is enjoying massive deluxe burgers and super-sized soft drinks. Old age seems a long way off, and there is that feeling that you have more "time" to get all of this together and take it seriously. But you don't. Your health down the road will be directly influenced by the decisions you make today.

Relax. You have a lot to learn in this area. While you are currently not getting enough sleep, you are also not allowing yourself to relax and regroup. You have the sense that 'to burn out for Christ' is a spiritual thing. But it isn't. He never asked you to do so. Make sure that you stay balanced. Understand that part of this balance involves relaxation. Find things that you enjoy doing that will take your mind off of the tasks at hand. The biblical principle of "Sabbath" is important. You need to take a day off from your schedule to allow your mind and body to rest. Relax. Regroup. Rethink. Otherwise, you will get to the place where you can no longer clearly discern things and you'll have problems seeing the bigger picture. Make sure you are taking at least one 24-hour period of time every week to rest. And then, make sure that you periodically take a vacation. You will rest the most and dream the biggest during your time off!

You won't go to hell for smoking you'll just smell like you've been there! Westernized Christianity demonizes certain vices while it overlooks others. I grew up with the idea that the smokers and the drinkers were all going to hell. I remember as a young child being afraid of a man who smoked outside after the church service. I made sure I stayed far away from him. Westernized Christianity says smoking is a spiritual problem, but overeating is not. You just have to attend a good ol' Church "pot luck" to understand that! Westernized Christianity says drinking alcohol is a sin. And yet, we serve multiple cups of highly caffeinated coffee in the lobby of most churches today. For many people, sin is in the eyes of the beholder. Smith Wigglesworth said "Sin is anything that cools my affection towards God." Good definition. Our lists usually consist of everything that bothers us about everyone else, and very few things that personally convict us. Again, it's all about people who sin differently than we do. Make sure you don't have a list. You'll miss the point. When your desire is to love unconditionally and leave judgment to God, it frees you to communicate with people without automatically seeing their sin. Just as Jesus separated our sin from our communication from God, you need to do the same thing in your communication with others.

Beware of Christian bullies! Seriously?! You would expect to find kind, compassionate, and easy-going people in the Christian faith. At least that's the ideal. But, as you are fully aware, the body of Christ is full of bullies. There are pastors who yell at their congregations. Many have their own agenda, and expect you to follow it. There will always be those people who try to bully you into believing what they believe, and do what they do. Some of those who don't agree with you will try to bully you with scripture taken completely out of context. They will gossip and bring you up in prayer meetings. But at the end of the day, it's all bullying. They are not healthy and they are certainly not your friends. They tell you your dreams are impossible. They do everything to keep the body of Christ from moving forward. In their minds, they believe they are right. But in reality, it's simple jealousy and confusion. What happens when a bully becomes a Christian? Many times they simply become Christian bullies. They have a need to control things, and in the end, they make you feel very small. You don't owe them anything. You don't have to follow them. You just have to be aware of them, and avoid them.

Money is an enormous issue. The Christian community is not shy in telling you how to spend your money. Church leaders have a lot to say based upon personal interpretation. "God wants you to give us your money." "Tithe 10% of your income." "The New Testament doesn't tell us to tithe." And, "the more you give, the more you will receive. You can't out-give God." Even though there is some truth in all of these statements, they can be misleading. Unfortunately, many people that give out of a need for a higher income are left with a want for more. In the end, you will have to decide which of these you will believe. I recommend you take it to God. Ask Him to show you what He wants you to do. Be open to His ongoing promptings in this area.

The heart of "giving" in the New Testament is emotional. The Bible tells us to give "Cheerfully." That is a strange word to describe giving unless you understand what giving is all about. Giving is directly connected to our relationship with God. When you have connected with Him, and His care and compassion become yours, giving will become a joy and a blessing. It becomes an extension of the heart of God. When your giving is motivated by a mandate instead of your heart, it becomes meaningless. Giving involves your compassion and love for others. You will find your balance in giving as you are motivated by the Holy Spirit's love inside of you to love God and others. Your money will follow your heart. If you are struggling with giving, it could be because you have not developed God's heart for people in distress. And again, this only happens when you fall in love with people as motivated by the Holy Spirit.

Don't feel entitled. God doesn't owe you money, nor does He owe you a living. Hard work and honest effort produce their own rewards. There are too many who simply sit back and wait for God to reward them, even though they haven't put in any effort. Don't be one of those who are constantly disappointed because God didn't magically provide for them. Living is difficult. God expects you to use wisdom.

Live within your means. "Downsizing" is an attitude and it requires reconsidering your current material situation. In practice, this could mean moving to a smaller place or getting rid of some of your clothing. You will be amazed at how little it takes to survive. If you continue to have an attitude of "downsizing" instead of accumulating more stuff, you will succeed in controlling your stuff, instead of allowing your stuff to control you. Don't use credit to live. If you can't afford something, you probably don't need it. Let me explain. When most people purchase a new car, they agree to make payments. Those payments also include interest. Over the life of the car, many will have paid for it twice. When you see something you desire, it is easy to simply put it on a credit card and worry about the payment another time. Many rack up huge debt on their credit cards, and a few months later, couldn't even tell you what 10% of those purchases were for!

Don't live on credit. Here's an example to consider: every time you buy a new vehicle, start a savings account for the next one. You can find a great used car for $10,000. You calculate that this car will last you for about 7 years. Begin to save for the next car immediately. If you can manage to save $1,000 per year ($83 per month), at the end of the 7 years, you will have enough cash for a new one. You can typically get $3,000 for your old car at that point. If you can simply plan ahead, you will end up saving a lot of money and you won't be in debt.

There are three questions you should ask yourself before purchasing anything:

1. Is this something I truly need? Does it fit with my lifestyle of being debt free and living with minimal possessions, or am I just adding to a larger collection?

2. Am I spending more money than I need to on this item? Could I buy it used and accomplish the same goals?

3. Am I emotionally attached to this item? If so, walk away. Come back when you can make a decision based on need instead of impulse.

4. Does it fit in with my plans for the future? Travel? Providing for your family? Schooling? When you know you are going to need something in the future, begin to save for it.

Your money involves responsibility. Once you understand the difference between "need" and "want" you will find freedom from your bondage to finances. It isn't just about you. Again, it is about all of those around you as well. When your own needs are in perspective, you will be able to help those around you a lot more.

Let go of your money. Many people fall into the pit of holding on to their money with everything they have. Our society says that our significance and our meaning come from finances. The more you have, the better off you are. But that simply isn't true. Some of the most miserable people in the world are wealthy. And some of the most joyful and peaceful are those that have very little. We hear it said that money can't buy you happiness. But I would go one step further. Happiness and money have nothing to do with each other! It's interesting when you hear the testimony of people who have won the lottery. All of a sudden, they've gone from having little money to great wealth. And they usually spend all the money in a short time. Friends and relatives who haven't spoken to them for years suddenly try to become their best friends. They have trouble knowing who to trust and what to trust. Their money becomes more of a curse than a blessing. Obviously, you're not winning the lottery. And you don't have to worry about dealing with large sums of money. But the principles are still there. Money is only a means to an end. Don't focus on it. Be free with it. Be generous. Give much of it away. Use it to bless others in need. Let go of it. Lift your bondage to it. Realize that the greatest gifts and the biggest blessings are free; they have been given to you by a very generous God who loves you very much.

God is faithful with finances. At this point, you are living mostly on faith. The projects you are working on have financial demands that are more than you can earn personally. You are beginning to see the necessity of going to Him with your needs. You will discover, as you grow older, that being financially dependent upon God (living in faith) is a big blessing. When you struggle for finances, it will be a good check and balance for you spiritually. Go to the Lord in prayer and listen. You will be told if you need to persevere, or if you need to correct or adjust something and change your path. God will work through your finances. Where He guides, He provides.

God the builder, yes He can! It's amazing to watch God bring resources together. Again, this is something you really haven't experienced yet. But you will find that it takes very little money to keep a ministry going. God has resources you don't know about. He has people that are ready to help. Again, when He asks you to do something and guides you in a certain direction, He will always take care of the details. Those details are really not up to you. They are up to Him.

What does "being a good steward" of your money look like? We assume that it has to do with investing and saving. We have visions of an old man counting his money and hoarding it. But that couldn't be further from the truth. In my experience, being a good steward is all about distribution. It's about knowing who needs finances and finding the best way to bless them. It's about helping people to help themselves. It's about investing in other's futures. It's really not so much about you, but about others. We hear a lot of pastors these days saying, "you can't out-give God!" And even though some of them are using this phrase as a gimmick to actually bring more money into their churches, the core concept is very true. God does have unlimited resources. And He will use those resources to bless those in need.

God has a plan, and He's going to fulfill it. He has chosen to use you in this process, whether you want to be part of it or not. He wants us to be blessed as we respond to those who truly need our help. The real key is to help people to help themselves. That involves some creativity and some involvement. You'll need to think outside the box!

Put your money where your heart is. So many are giving simply because they feel they are supposed to. They carefully count out 10% of their paycheck, and resentfully pay their tithe. But this is not at all what God had in mind. When your heart motivates your giving, it isn't a bitter experience. Instead, you will feel cheerful when you give because your finances are attached to your desire to give and please God.

SEXUAL

"The truth is, God Invented Sex! It was God's idea."
DR. STEVE HIGHLANDER

This is a difficult letter to write. Mostly because it is intensely personal. Sex has been called a "gift." But you may not agree with that at 21. Being unmarried, it may seem like more of a curse. Others would say it is an "achievement." The trick is to stay celibate until you are married. You might say it is a "burden." A burden that seems way too heavy most of the time. What was God thinking?

Sex was God's idea in the first place. Seriously?! That may feel a little disturbing to you, since most guys your age would consider it a cross to bear. So I ask you to consider this: If it was God's idea, and He meant it for good, then there must be something more to it, right?

What should sexuality look like at 21? How do you shake that feeling that you are somehow "missing something?" The dots don't seem to connect. You feel driven. But none of the drive seems spiritual, or even moral. You struggle to keep your eyes to yourself. You try hard not to think "bad thoughts" about that beautiful girl standing next to you in church. You feel out of control. Inappropriate. A pervert. But wait... did you say this was "God's idea? Yes, it was/is God's idea. And you will struggle with working through your hormones to discover the beauty of God's idea.

Sexual issues and challenges follow us into almost every area of life. Maybe you are feeling euphoria attached to the current "love of your life" or, you are trying to recover from that special one that simply doesn't love you back. It could be that longing for someone to complete your life. Whew! It's a challenge just controlling your sexual appetite! What you need to know is this: It's all connected! When you work through the challenges and make sense of all of this, you will quickly go from sexual to spiritual. That is ultimately where it all makes sense. And so, we will begin there.

God began the process with Adam and Eve. He gave them to each other, and they began the celebration of love and total commitment. He could have made the procreation process very mechanical and very unfeeling. But that was not His idea. He chose for the act of lovemaking to be an explosion of emotion, desire, commitment, and family. Children are conceived and born as a result of intimacy. And so, sexual contact becomes a most intimate act that lays a foundation of deep love as the foundation for family.

But you are still single. How can this possibly apply to you? While it is true that sexuality can only ultimately be understood in marriage, it is also true that your body doesn't wait until then. Puberty is an event, not a choice. Whether you feel ready or not (and most of us don't!), your body explodes with a whole arsenal of sexual feelings, triggers, and emotions. It seems to happen overnight and usually leaves you confused and a bit concerned. And of course, there is usually no one to talk to about this. So you go with so many questions in your mind, and do your best to figure out the answers on your own.

The Church usually makes it worse. Pastors and youth leaders are notorious for talking about the sins of sex and lust, without truly defining them or explaining the differences. You grow up feeling even more confused, and now condemned. Surely you are doing something wrong. Surely God must be angry with you. If people only knew some of the things you think and fantasize about, they would be shocked! Everyone would hate you. So you suffer in silence. You know "it's" wrong (whatever "it" is). You feel guilty. Just guilty!

Sex verses lust. The Bible has surprisingly little to say about the mechanics of sex, but a whole lot to say about lust. That point alone is an excellent place to begin to answer this complex question. Any gift God gives you can be distorted and used in a negative, self-serving way. Sex is no different. And, since it is also connected to such a powerful physical and emotional drive, it seems even more monumental to figure it out. If sex is a gift from God, and part of His plan, then we should not view it as a curse. It can only be a blessing. So it is with any gift God gives us. And as a blessing, it isn't a matter of trying to suppress it or "praying it away," but rather a matter of managing it with commitment, sensitivity, and grace. Again, everyone is different. For some, this might include masturbation (as long as lust is not involved). For others it may be nocturnal emissions (wet dreams). The Bible is surprisingly silent on these things. Why? Because they are not an issue, they are normal. The issue is lust, and lust will always be your enemy. If you google "lust," almost 100 references from all over the Bible will instantly pop up. God isn't silent about how He feels about this controversial subject.

Porn addiction isn't sex. It is a cheap imitation, not the real thing. While it is true that most guys masturbate while watching porn, it doesn't necessarily mean the two are connected. Lust takes the "gift" part out of sexuality. It becomes something it was never intended to be. Dr. Norman Doidge, in his book *The Brain That Changes Itself*, describes how pornography causes rewiring of the neural circuits. In a *study of men viewing internet pornography, the men looked "uncannily" like rats pushing the levers in experimental Skinner boxes. "Like the addicted rats,"* Dr Doidge points out, *"the men were desperately seeking their next fix, clicking the mouse just as the rats pushed the lever."* All addictions, Dr. Doidge goes on to tell us, cause *"lifelong, neuroplastic changes in the brain. This includes porn addiction. Dopamine is also involved in plastic change. The same surge of dopamine that thrills us also consolidates neuronal connections. An important link with porn is that dopamine is also released in sexual excitement, increasing the sex drive in both sexes, facilitating orgasm, and activating the brain's pleasure centers. Hence the addictive power of pornography. The men at their computers looking at porn were uncannily like the rats in the cages of the NIH, pressing the bar to get a shot of dopamine or its equivalent. Though they didn't know it, they had been seduced into pornographic training sessions that met all the conditions required for plastic change of brain maps. Since neurons that fire together wire together, these men got massive amounts of practice wiring these images into the pleasure centers of the brain, with the rapt attention necessary for plastic change. They imagined these images when away from their computers, or while having sex with their girlfriends, reinforcing them. Each time they felt sexual excitement and had an orgasm when they masturbated, a "spritz of dopamine," the reward neurotransmitter, consolidated the connections made in the brain during the sessions. It is in this way that pornography becomes a serious addiction, comparable to heroin or crack cocaine addiction, and begins its slow and deadly assault on the brain. And as other research has shown, it facilitates callousness in sexual relationships—sex completely divorced from love and an interest in family and children."*

You have some decisions to make about your sexuality. As you can see, this is a complex subject. It will take some research, some prayer, and some honest communication with other guys who are willing to also be honest about their own sexual standards. But no matter what, always remember that the expression of your sexuality is personal. It is not to be shared with anyone else until you get married. Its future purpose is only fully realized in a loving, committed relationship with someone you will call "your wife."

The most important sex organ you have is your brain. That's where it all begins. There are so many messages being thrown at you these days. Society expects you to experiment sexually. You are expected to become self-educated by creating your own experiences. Naivety is considered immature. But actually, it's not. You will never have to be an expert in this field. Marriage is an excellent school. Marriage provides a great paradigm for exploring and experiencing with your sexuality. You can learn together with the person you love the most and have an emotional and mental connection with—your wife. Inside the paradigm of marriage you have security, freedom, and trust.

"Sex" and "lust" are two words that are misunderstood and need some clarification. The church has a tendency to condemn them interchangeably. We are left with the feeling that sex is a dirty word, and lust is somehow connected. Again, if sex was God's idea, then there must be a standard here that is foundational and good. Sex is about expression. It is about personal intimacy in a moral and committed setting. At puberty it becomes one more attribute of who you are and who you are becoming. And then, in marriage, another person is added to your expression of sexuality. The moral ideal for a lifetime is to follow in this progression.

Lust, on the other hand, wants to play outside the lines. It is selfish and desires satisfaction without commitment or morality. It's focus is on cheap thrills instead of a deeper moral commitment. Lust overrides the "warnings" going off in your head and convinces you that temporary pleasure is exciting and stimulating. And that's true. But then there are the consequences. It is easy for sex in a relationship to become lust when the love in the relationship dies. Song of Solomon in the Bible is a whole book about healthy sexual desire. But, as history teaches us, Solomon somehow forgot his commitment to this woman he was so in love with, and started to allow lust to take over. The Bible tells us that at one point he had 400 wives and 600 live-in girlfriends. Even the wisest man in the world can fall. The important thing is to keep love alive in any relationship, and to remember that lust is the enemy of love.

Your personal sexuality is between you and God alone. Don't share it with anyone else. Make sure you don't use porn or other people to express it before marriage. Porn will ruin your view on women and sexuality in general. Besides that, by watching porn you are contributing to an industry that degrades and exploits women. This ruins thousands of marriages every year. Your biggest gift to your wife will be your virginity. Keep it, and make sure that you do everything in your power to fight for it. Don't give in to peer pressure or to your own lustful desires. Remember, your personal sexuality is just that: Personal.

Marriage or celibacy? This is something you're thinking about right now, and it's a decision that will affect your whole life. All these thoughts are running through your head: "Which is more Biblical? Which is more fulfilling?" Take your time with it. You really don't have to run toward a decision at all! Love can emerge when you least expect it. So many people give up on love altogether, only to find "that special someone" by surprise. Marriage is amazing. One of the most wonderful ministries you can ever have is that of being a husband and a father. It's a very high calling and you would totally enjoy this option. But, it isn't for everyone. There are some that God calls to celibacy, to remain a virgin, and unmarried. And, it's not the end of the world. It isn't contagious, and it won't kill you. For some, it's the best option and it won't feel like a sacrifice. You are not a martyr. If that becomes your impression, than perhaps celibacy is not for you. However, marriage just may not be your ticket to fulfillment! If you do remain celibate, you must surround yourself with people who can complete you. Remember, an unmarried man is not complete. There are perspectives that you don't have. There are feelings that you don't experience. Women experience emotions differently than men and those experiences are shared between a man and wife in marriage. But as a single man you still need the balance of the female experiences in your life. Make sure that you always have good female friends around you, who can speak into your life.

SOCIAL

"I cannot even imagine where I would be today were it not for that handful of friends who have given me a heart full of joy."
CHARLES R. SWINDOLL

You have a lot to learn about friendships. This is a subject that I have learned to feel very strongly about. Sadly, it's one that you don't understand very well at this point. There are basically three kinds of friendships...

1. **Casual Friends:** Most of your friends will fall in this category. They may be great people to hang out with, but they won't necessarily fulfill any deeper need that you might have. These friends will come and go. As a result, you won't feel the need to see them regularly.

2. **Close Friends:** These are people with whom you establish a connection. They can speak into your life if you let them. Hold onto these. If you'll allow yourself to listen and learn from them, they will make a difference in your life.

3. **Intimate Friends:** These friends will be few. You may only have one or two of them in your lifetime. Listen to your

intimate friends input when you fall in love. When you're seeking direction in life. When your world falls apart. These intimate friends know you well and have earned the right to speak into your life. They are trustworthy. They will help guide your spiritual life and will be significant in identifying your spiritual gifts and direction. Your intimate friends need to be emotionally stable. You can have chronically emotionally unstable friends in your close circle, but not as intimate friends. That closeness would make such a friend a project—not a person who helps balance you. Intimate friends are not in competition with you. They are your equal. They walk beside you. They listen to you. They speak honestly with you. They understand you. Their friendship and behaviors are reciprocal. As you or they waft in and out of good times, hard times, and temporary instability, you are there for each other.

Keep healthy boundaries. Friendships are difficult at best. Because you love people, you have a true desire to help them. But many times that can get you into a lot of trouble. You're not as strong as you think you are. Many around you are struggling with moral and spiritual issues, and will continue to make unwise decisions. Not everyone wants your guidance. Listen intensely to God's spirit inside of you as He leads you to specific individuals. There are those who really desire your help, and will listen to you. There are so many others who won't. Instead of using your energy trying to help everyone, focus your energy on those who really need and want your interaction.

Deeper friendships with the opposite sex can be tricky! This is an important area for honest and strong boundaries. Men and women were created to be attracted to each other. You can't change that. It's just the way you are built. When a relationship with anyone becomes deeper, it opens the door to emotions. In a relationship with someone of the opposite sex, emotions need to be monitored. It is a vulnerable place for both of you. Many guys have failed here and you are one of them. Honesty is difficult for both men and women when feelings get in the way. Be protective of her heart and aware of her emotions. Opposite sex friendships need to be void of "those kinds" of feelings for either of you. You may only have a handful of close female friends your whole life. Guard their emotions. If they are married make sure their husbands are also your friends. And never step in and counsel her about her personal relationships. Always choose to be her friend, not her rescuer.

Allow yourself to be nurtured. You don't have to simply keep going and push through your difficulties. There are caring people around you who would like to help. You're good at nurturing others, but you have a difficult time allowing others into your life. Your walls go up, and you become way too private. You need to allow others to have spiritual and emotional input into your life. There are those that will be a great help to you if you allow them to. You have this feeling that others won't like you if they really get to know you. You feel you need to keep a distance so that people will continue to respect you. But in reality, people will respect you more if you open up and become more transparent. Don't be afraid of it. It's liberating and it's honest.

Make sure you pay attention to people around you. So many seem to live in a bubble. They avoid making eye contact as they walk by you. They don't smile. They keep to themselves. It seems as if they just want to be left alone. But that is rarely the case. Most people are waiting for someone else to make the first move. They wait for your smile, so they can smile back. They wait for you to ask a question so they can engage in conversation. Most don't want to be presumptuous and begin a conversation with "strangers." But in reality, there are no strangers. There are only people with whom you have not yet started a conversation. I imagine we are going to spend eternity doing just that. We might as well get started now!

Allow Jesus' compassion to consume you. This is one of the biggest lessons you have yet to learn. When you believe in a project it's easy to get involved. It's even easier to get involved with things for which you have a heart. But your efforts have a limit. Unless you allow the Lord's compassion for people to motivate you, you'll find yourself making decisions that are not always in the best interest of others. Your friendships and family will suffer if you have limited compassion. Your natural compassion is based on your feelings, and on your endurance. God's supernatural compassion is unconditional and unending. It's an amazing thing to begin to love people unconditionally. The more His compassion flows through you; it becomes very evident that it's not from you, but from Him. It's an awesome thing to be able to work from the heart of God.

It is important that you make lasting friends. These days everything seems so temporary. Friends come and go. When you ask someone how many friends they have, they assume you are talking about their friend list on Facebook. We have substituted social media for honest personal connection with people. This is your problem at 21. You formalize your contacts. You compartmentalize your relationships. You surround yourself with people but you limit communication. As a result, you are lonely. You are not open with people on a deeper level. There are those people who will hang on to your friendship because they care about you. In the future those people will be the most special people in your life. But you have yet to learn the true value of friendship. You have yet to become vulnerable enough to have deep friendships. Appreciate your friends, prioritize time with them, and hold on to them.

Don't limit your friendship to Christians only. Many of your most painful times in the future will result from Christian friends who betray you. Many of them are people you trust simply because they are Christians. These betrayals are the ones that hurt the most! Make sure you make friendships from the heart. Find people you feel a connection with and let them into your life. There are some amazing people out there who will enrich your life greatly who are not Christians... yet.

You will always have difficult people around you. Get used to it. There are some people who have difficult lives, and as a result, they become fairly toxic. It doesn't mean they're not worth the friendship. It simply means that they need a little more care and communication. Don't write people off just because they're difficult. You can be a little difficult at times as well. The key to any friendship is communication. Talk. Talk again. Then talk some more. Most things can be resolved when we make the effort to understand each other and come to a mutual agreement. Don't be too quick to dispose of friendships when they become difficult. You'll find that some of your greatest friendships were very difficult at first. Keep trying.

You will always have critics. There will always be people who criticize your faith and your walk with the Lord. Many will tell you that because you believe in God, you're not a free thinker. Others will challenge the validity of the Bible. Others will challenge the historic accounts of Jesus. As you grow older you'll have better and more thorough answers for many of these people. However, you'll find that most of these people are not really seeking answers to these questions; their seeking goes beyond this. Most people really desire to find truth and meaning for their life. That's why it's so important to transparently live your life in front of people. When you are open with your life, then people begin to ask about the hope that you have within you. As you become more deeply connected in your relationship with Jesus, you'll find that more and more people will seek after the hope you have. It isn't about how many of their theological or sociological questions you can answer, but rather, how you answer the questions of their hearts.

Celebrate diversity! There are so many different kinds of people. And, as a result, there are so many different kinds of Christians. You're involved in rock 'n roll. That's your passion. Because that music is your passion, you tend to close your heart to other kinds of music ministries. It's difficult for you to understand how God could possibly use Christian Country Western music simply because you don't like it. One of the greatest surprises in your future will be that you have more in common with many of those "different" people than you thought. There are so many who will enrich your life and who are not involved with your particular passions. Their involvement with you is so important. It's easy for you to become shortsighted. You have specific goals and dreams. And because you're so driven, you don't always see what God is doing in other areas. Make sure you become involved with the whole body of Christ, and not just a part of it. Come up for air once in a while, and see what the rest of the Christian community is up to!

Learn the difference between entertainment and meaningful encounters. One of the things that bothers you at 21 is the state of the church and the way it views ministry with young people. You find that the average youth group leader focuses on entertaining young people, just to keep them coming to church. I am glad that bothers you. I encourage you to continue to feel this way. As these kids finish school and leave home, the dropout rate of their participation in the body of Christ is huge—which means that they didn't feel anything of substance to take with them. All of those years of entertaining them and trying not to offend them, in the long run, will not pay off. What they really want is meaningful encounters. They need to figure out their passions and who they are. To do that they need quality time with those who are older and more mature. They need to dialogue about their questions and they need opportunities to experience difficulties together to glean from each other and their role models. In short, they need to be exposed to and experience real life lessons to prepare them for real life on their own. Most of them will not find their time in church relevant to their future. They will simply leave it behind as they move on. Continue to be committed to honesty, transparency, and real dialogue. Continue to speak to life's issues and its concerns. Talk about faith, pain, frustration, confusion, and decision-making. These are the real issues. These are the areas that young people really need to talk about. Don't let them down by simply supplying them with entertainment. The younger generation around you will thank you for it later.

Choose to have quality time. There are so many things happening in the world today. You have so many choices. And the demands that are made of you will leave you empty and unfulfilled. Choose wisely when dealing with things that will give you a quality life. Many people believe that to be a good Christian, you have to attend church every time the doors are open. Sunday morning, Sunday evening, Wednesday night prayer meeting, youth group on the weekend, etc. Pastors need to stay aware of the demands this makes on individuals and families. They need to encourage people to find the best fit for them and their family. Pastors should also encourage people to spend quality time with their families. The same is true for you with your work, your relationships, and your ministry. You can't say "yes" to everything. You shouldn't say "yes" to everything. If you are stretched too thin, you won't give quality time to anything. Choose wisely!

Loneliness is usually not a friend issue. Most people naturally assume that if you feel lonely, it's because you don't have any friends. But loneliness has very little to do with friendships. There are many who are surrounded by people all the time and are still very lonely. There is a big difference between "being alone" and "feeling lonely." Loneliness usually has more to do with your connection with God than anything else. God is your first resource. Obviously, people do complete your life. You'll feel more loved and encouraged as a result of close relationships. But they can't cure loneliness. That is a God issue. Go to God in prayer. Realize that He already understands the problems and knows the solutions. It isn't just that you need to tell Him how you feel (although that's important for your personal processing), but you also need to listen to His heart. That emptiness that you feel needs to find a remedy. God is the remedy. Be sure you spend enough time finding God's agenda. Always check yourself to make sure you're on the right track. Loneliness, for you, is usually a red flag telling you that you're getting off course. God will speak through your emotions. Many times it's the only way He can get through to you!

Don't marry out of loneliness. Many hurry into relationships. They fall "in love" easily. And then they fall "out of love" just as easily. Nothing feels more lonely than being in the middle of a relationship with someone who doesn't love or understand you. The cure for loneliness is not marriage.

Hate the sin, love the sinner. Seriously?! You don't even think that's possible! Your mind has a very difficult time separating those two emotions. They are so radically opposed to each other. Jesus laid some very basic groundwork for our thinking process; "You have heard that it was said, 'Love your neighbor and hate your enemy. But I tell you, love your enemies and pray for those who persecute you, that you may be children of your Father in heaven. He causes His sun to rise on the evil and the good, and sends rain on the righteous and the unrighteous. If you love those who love you, what reward will you get? Are not even the tax collectors doing that? And if you greet only your own people, what are you doing more than others? Do not pagans do that? (Matthew 5:43-47 NIV). You have a desire to love people, but at this point in your life, you are too selective. You find it easy to love people who love you back. But you struggle loving those who don't reciprocate.

Jesus' actions and words seem to pose a dilemma. What do you do with those who are more difficult to love? What about the people that rub you the wrong way or those who make your life miserable? What about those who are not committed to the same moral standards about sexuality, child rearing, politics… whew! The list goes on and on. And outside biblical standards, who is to say your ideals are the right ideals? There are 'truths' in which you believe now, that you will not believe in the future.

Again, we are told to hate sin, but love those who sin. And you resemble the remark, 'those who sin'. You want to be loved even when you sin. But you need to do that for others. After all these years, I have never been able to separate the two. I have to take sin out of the equation. Christ is telling you in this portion of scripture to love. Love unconditionally! Love even those who are difficult to love. When you begin to love with Christ's love, the whole "sin" problem disappears. Instead of seeing sin, you see past it. You see a person. You begin to understand their hurt and motivations.

As long as you are judging people according to their sins, you will never love others with a pure heart. "Hate the sin, love the sinner," was not meant for you to adopt a philosophy that those who sin differently than you have sin that is worse than yours. Sin doesn't fall into different categories, as if sin even has categories. Sin is sin. If you could see your personal sin from Christ's perspective on the cross, you would change your judgment of others in a heartbeat. If you could view Christ as He reads through the list of your offenses, your face would turn red with embarrassment and your heart would fill with discouragement. But Christ looks you straight in the eyes, and tells you He loves you unconditionally in spite of your sins. He did the unspeakable. He died for you! "Greater love has no one than this, that one lay down his life for his friends." (John 15:13 NASB) Jesus knew love would be the greatest motivator and the best foundation for reformation. Again, that's why He summed up all the commandments in the Bible into six words: Love God. Love Others. Love Yourself. "Love the Lord your **God** with all your heart and with all your soul and with all your strength and with all your mind'; and, 'Love your **neighbor** as **yourself**." (Luke 10:27 NIV) So, instead of allowing yourself to focus on the sin in someone else's life, why don't you just concentrate on hating the sin in your own life and loving others unconditionally!

Sometimes, bad things happen to "good Christians." You have this feeling that as long as you're on the right track, nothing bad will happen. That's not true. All of us go through difficulties. All of us are mistreated from time to time. No one lives a perfect life. This concept is not only difficult for you, it's also very difficult for people around you. Some believe if you're a Christian or a good person, that life should be a lot easier. Life should somehow owe you an easier existence if you're "good". At the root of these feelings is our limited philosophy that good people deserve good things and bad people deserve bad things. We don't get so upset when bad things happen to bad people. But we do get upset when good things happen to bad people. Conversely, we want good things to happen to good people. At 21, it seems that good things embrace people who don't deserve it, while the ones who are good in character are left with nothing but sadness and pain. You note that it rains on the just and the unjust alike. These are deep issues. And issues worth pondering. But, in the moments you find yourself needing to rest and rely on God in a crisis remember, God never promises an easy life. He promises to be there no matter what happens. And He promises that, even though there's a storm around you, He will give you His peace.

Don't allow bitterness to sneak up on you. Because you are an emotional person, it is easy to take everything personally. When people disagree with you and challenge you, it feels like a personal attack. You have a difficult time checking your heart and your emotions with those people. Not only that, but you struggle with allowing a "root of bitterness" to grow as a result. There is a good reason the Bible speaks about bitterness. *"Look after each other so that none of you fails to receive the grace of God. Watch out that no poisonous root of bitterness grows up to trouble you, corrupting many."* (Hebrews 12:15 NLT) Here is the key: Look after each other! It is very difficult to get rid of bitterness yourself. Your emotions will always get in the way. You need help from trustworthy friends. You don't need to rant about how horrible the situation is and how much you have been mistreated. Instead, you need to get to the point of forgiveness. That is what the "grace" part in this scripture is talking about. Something amazing happens to your heart when you pray for someone with whom you are at odds. That prayer is not, "Lord, forgive them for what they have done to me!" But rather, "Lord, change my heart to give me unconditional love toward this person. Allow me to see them through your eyes. Allow me to feel what they feel. Allow me to understand. And, forgive me for my part in the misunderstanding, even if it is not completely clear to me now."

Realize that a root of bitterness inside of you will corrupt many.
There will always be those people in your life who love you and will
"defend" you. They will adopt your bitterness toward another person.
That's the point of the above scripture when it says, *"Watch out that
no poisonous root of bitterness grows up to trouble you, corrupting many."*
This really is a big deal. You need to model forgiveness to others. Otherwise, how will people who look to you for guidance and advice learn
to forgive? Most of our moral character comes from imitating others
with those same character traits. People around you will either copy
your bitterness, and feel justified in their own bitterness, or they will
copy your forgiveness and choose to walk in God's grace.

Your root is your root. When bitterness takes over, it infects everything else in your life. That's why the Bible uses this word "root" to describe bitterness. Because it is at the very bottom of everything else it will infect every area of your life. You will discover that it affects the way you love and forgive others in your life. It will cloud your understanding of God's grace. And, most of all, it will affect your relationship with God. Why? Because He will always remind you that you have a root of bitterness "festering." He knows that you have to move past it to stay in harmony in your relationship with Him and with others.

Create good honest fellowship. Once you are able to have honest communication with yourself and with God, you become better equipped to work with people! I hope you understand by now that a deeper connection with others isn't truly possible until you have laid the basic foundation for friendship. People will only go as deeply with you as you are able to go and will allow. People need to feel comfortable so they can be honest and transparent. Otherwise, your friendships are doomed to remain casual and temporary. This does not mean that your life has to be lived as an open book. It's okay to be private and keep boundaries on what you want to share with your friends. But you still need to be honest about the things you do share. Many people are emotionally disconnected, and they assume that others around them are as well. When you are able to take someone deeper in their relationship with you, you give them—and you—a priceless gift.

This is the kind of fellowship God intended for His church. His desire is for us to be caring, nurturing, and honest. Most people are afraid of this. You are one of them. And, as I have mentioned before, it is only when you have peace with yourself and with God, that you are changed. As the church (believers together in fellowship) begin to risk vulnerability with each other, they begin to honestly understand the heart of Christ. Use your spiritual gifts and understand what is needed on a deeper level. You will become less critical and more encouraging. Remember, the biblical church is not a building. Church is simply Christians coming together. Sharing. Encouraging. Using their spiritual gifts, etc. In the early church, people felt comfortable meeting in their homes and common places. In fact, Acts 2:42-47 describes this early brotherhood in more detail. Christians were connected. When you really feel connected with someone, you desire the best for them. You have their back, and they have yours. It is at this point that you become equally yoked.

Most Churches teach friendship evangelism. They tell you to become a friend to someone first, and then share the Gospel with them. Don't fall into that trap of thinking. Put yourself in the position of others. If you knew that someone was only becoming your friend for the sake of converting you to their religion, it would make you feel bad. Why is it that we continue to use gimmicks to win people to Christ? Really, it isn't so much about "earning the right to be heard" as it is about being a "real" friend. There are many who fall away from the church after they are converted because all of their "friends" are busy becoming new "friends" to other non-Christians. For this reason, many feel lonelier after they become Christians than they did before they were saved.

You have a lot to learn about unlimited love and friendship. Friendships should not be developed solely because of your agenda(s). Foundations for friendships should never be agenda driven. Loving the other person unconditionally should be the foundation for friendship. Remember that people are not as impressed by your words as they are about your honestly and transparency. If you become that kind of a friend, you will likely find it is a two way street. Unlimited love towards a friend will mean so much to the friend. In the end you will receive so much more!

Socratic discussion. At this point in my life, I am not a fan of this "Spectator sport" we call organized church. By that, I mean one person speaking while everyone else watches. It's not a New Testament model. You are still very much involved in tradition, even though you think you're being very innovative and forward thinking. But you're going to learn that there is a whole lot more to communication than simply listening to someone speak. Personal relationships and small group dynamics are so important. Socratic discussion has become the foundation of my leadership model. It can best be defined as a discussion process during which a facilitator promotes independent, reflective, and critical thinking within a small group of people. And its foundation, once again, has to do with honestly living your life in front of people. This gives them an answer for the hope they see that you have within you and allows your life and your ideals to actually challenge others in theirs. It has become the joy of my life to listen more than I speak, and to allow others to come to their own conclusions. When you simply tell someone what to believe, it goes in one ear and out the other. But, when a person is involved in the process of discovery, they own the answers as well. It makes such a difference! Don't let your ego get in the way of the process. It is less important what you say and more important that you let people develop their own healthy conclusions.

God is large and in charge! It's easy to become discouraged by politics, people's agendas, and the general state of the world. Every generation feels the things arund them are out of control. We see atrocities and the miscommunication internationally. It's easy to feel gloom and doom. It's easy to feel defeated. But the God we serve is not defeated. God is bigger than any circumstance. He is bigger than any atrocity. God revives what is dead and brings new possibilities to situations that seemed impossible. It's easy to get off track in your personal life and in your ministry when you feel defeated by situations in the world today. But make sure you don't focus on them. Keep your focus on the Lord. See the bigger picture. Many Christians around you will become politically motivated. Some will insist that God wants certain people in political offices. Others will fight the government; join in protest marches and/or demonstrations sounding the alarm for political change. But politics are ever changing, and regimes will come and go. The only thing that really matters in the end is building the kingdom of God. Be very careful that your contribution to the building of God's kingdom is spiritual and not political. With God, you can expect the unexpected.

Pray for revival. Gypsy Smith, a 19th-century revivalist, was once asked how to start revival. He explained that whenever he entered a new town to begin to preach the Gospel, he would draw a circle on the ground. Then he'd stand inside that circle and say, "O God, please send a revival to this town, and let it begin inside this circle." That's great advice! When revival breaks out inside the circle, it will have a ripple effect on everyone outside the circle. It begins with you! You don't create revival. You become revival. When your heart is changed and you're excited about your faith in Jesus Christ, then others will get excited as well.

Prayer doesn't change things. What? That's right! Prayer doesn't change things. Prayer changes people. And people change things. So many around you are caught up in praying for situations that need someone's intervention. I can just imagine someone sitting at home praying, "Lord, please bless the homeless on the streets tonight, and make sure they are safe and well fed." And God says, "Let's begin by giving you a heart for the homeless so that they become your passion and burden. Then you will personally be involved in their lives and see to it that they receive excellent care." You see, God needs to change your heart for people and situations before any change comes about. What if it's a situation where you are not able personally able to help? Pray specifically for those who are already working in the area you have a burden for. Focus on people touching the lives of other people. Explore the possibilities that *you* may be the person God is sending! You are His hands. His feet. His ears. His heart.

CONCLUSION

After all these years, what has been the most profound thing that I have learned? That's easy. It is my true understanding of the Holy Spirit. That is the most important thing I would pass along to you. Realizing that the Holy Spirit lives inside of you, and that He works from the inside out is life-changing. Instead of wandering around trying to find God everywhere, realize that He is right there inside of you! Jesus' promise of the coming Holy Spirit (John 7:37-39 PHILLIPS) was very specific. He said the Holy Spirit would be like "… rivers of living water flowing from your innermost heart." And then, a short time later, He died on the cross. At that moment, the curtain that separated the "Holy of Holies" from the rest of the temple was torn in half, from the top to the bottom. God removed the barrier. No longer is a high priest required to go through all the ceremonial cleansing to present your sins before God for forgiveness. God chose to relate to you personally. Jesus, your high priest, is now your advocate. But wait. It gets even better! The Bible tells us that the "Holy of Holies" has now been moved to a new location: INSIDE OF YOU! Amazing as it may be, you are now the "Temple of the Holy

Spirit." "Do you not know that your bodies are temples of the Holy Spirit, who is in you, whom you have received from God?" (1 Corinthians 6:19 NIV) That is a game-changer! God lives inside of you! You don't have to wander around aimlessly trying to find God somewhere in the cosmos, He has given you His exact location. He is always there. And that's why He can promise you, "I will never leave you nor forsake you." (Hebrews 13:5) You see, this defines who He is, and instructs you how to listen. And when you understand this principle and learn how to listen, it will change your life!

PASTOR BOB ONLINE

HOME PAGE:
http://PastorBobBeeman.com

YOUTUBE:
http://youtube.com/PastorBobBeeman

FACEBOOK:
https://www.facebook.com/PastorBob

TWITTER:
https://twitter.com/PastorBobBeeman

INSTAGRAM:
http://instagram.com/PastorBobBeeman

SPOTIFY:
PastorBobBeeman

Made in the USA
Lexington, KY
24 February 2015